A GUIDE TO PSYCHOTHERAPY IN IRELAND

IRISH COUNCIL FOR PSYCHOTHERAPY

A Guide to
Psychotherapy
in Ireland
New Revised Edition

the columba press

This edition published in 1998

First published in 1997 by

ᴄhe ᴄoᴌᴜᴍʙᴀ ᴘʀᴇꜱꜱ

55ᴀ Spruce Avenue, Stillorgan Industrial Park,
Blackrock, Co Dublin

Cover by Bill Bolger
Origination by The Columba Press
Printed in Ireland by Colour Books Ltd., Dublin

ISBN 1 85607 233 9

Contents

EXECUTIVE COMMITTEE OF
THE IRISH COUNCIL FOR PSYCHOTHERAPY

EDMUND MC HALE
Chair

ELLEN O'MALLEY-DUNLOP
Honorary Secretary

TOM BREEN
Honorary Treasurer

JANE BAIRD
ICPA

BARBARA FITZGERALD
IAHIP

AIDAN LAWLOR
CBT

PAULA LAWLOR
CBT

GODFREY O'DONNELL
ICPA

ANNE RICHARDSON
FTAI

MARY-PAULA WALSH
IAHIP

HONORARY MEMBERS
MICHAEL FITZGERALD
GER MURPHY
RUTH O'DONNELL

Contact address: Irish Council for Psychotherapy
17, Dame Court
Dublin 2.
Telephone: (01) 6794055
Fax: (01) 6797712

ABBREVIATIONS FOR ORGANISATIONS

CBT	Cognitive Behavioural Therapy
FTAI	Family Therapy Association of Ireland
IAHIP	Irish Association of Humanistic and Integrative Psychotherapy
ICPA	Irish Constructivist Psychotherapy Association
IFCAP	The Irish Forum for Child and Adolescent Psychotherapy
IFPP	The Irish Forum for Psychoanalytic Psychotherapy
IGAS	Irish Group Analytic Society

Introduction

While psychotherapy dates back to Sigmund Freud and his then radical innovations in Vienna one hundred years ago, its introduction to Ireland has been more recent. With the exception of one long established psychoanalytic practice in Monkstown, Co Dublin, the first psychotherapy services were introduced to Ireland less than twenty years ago. As this second edition of the Guide demonstrates, the growth of the field since then has been remarkable, with a steadily increasing number of practitioners, psychotherapy services and training programmes coming into existence.

Accompanying this growth in numbers and services, psychotherapists have been active in regulating their new profession to safeguard public interest and to promote continued self-examination and improvements of their standards. The Irish Council for Psychotherapy contains five sections which represent different approaches within the psychotherapy field. They are:

> Cognitive and Behavioural Therapy
> Constructivist Psychotherapy
> Couple and Family Therapy
> Humanistic and Integrative Psychotherapy
> Psychoanalytic Psychotherapy

This Guide contains a brief description of each approach which will identify some of the differences between them, but comparative research studies and the accumulated wisdom in the field indicate that psychotherapists of different orientations may have more in common in the manner in which they work than they have differences. Personal and relational factors such as trust, empathy and listening skills consistently emerge among the most significant aspects of the process.

It is important that people seeking assistance with personal concerns or problems should be able to obtain some assurance regarding the competence and integrity of those in whom they place their trust. Each of the five sections has their own organisational structure, training standards, code of ethics and complaints procedure. The Register provides the names of professionals who have committed themselves to the depth of training and high standards of professional conduct required by their section.

While there has been considerable growth in the field of psychotherapy throughout Europe, some confusion is often evident regarding distinctions between it and related professions such as psychiatry and psychology. Psychiatrists and Clinical Psychologists may undertake additional training to become Psychotherapists, but the prescribing of drugs or the psychometric assessment of individuals is not part of a psychotherapy process. If considered appropriate, a psychotherapist could refer a client elsewhere for these services. Psychotherapy is designed to help people to resolve or manage their difficulties in a collaborative relationship. One or more perspectives may be included in this exploration, including how they, and others who are significant in their lives, make sense of the difficulty and related issues, by examining what they and others do or how they relate, by exploring internal emotional states or by uncovering unconscious inner conflicts. The various approaches are described in greater detail as an introduction to each section in this Guide.

The European Association of Psychotherapy, of which the Irish Council for Psychotherapy is a member, has developed a European Certificate of Training in conjunction with the European Commission, which promotes the recognition of common standards of training for psychotherapists throughout Europe, and which will ensure their mobility across member states. While the European Commission does not have power to legally implement the certificate before it is adopted by member states, they have recommended it to the national co-ordinators of member states, and welcome it as an initiative in establishing joint platforms which will facilitate the employment of migrants within the European Union. The fact that training in psychotherapy, leading to the awarding of this certificate, is open to members of a wide range of other professions, is seen as an additional advantage by them.

The European certificate and this Guide will, hopefully, provide a useful source of reference for those people who wish to know more about psychotherapy, and particularly for those who may be considering using the services of an appropriately trained and ethical and responsible professional in addressing issues in their personal lives and relationships.

ED MC HALE, MA, PhD, MFT
CHAIR ELECT

Ethical Guidelines of
The European Association for Psychotherapy

The present ethical guidelines were prepared by the standing advisory Ethics-Group of the EAP 1993-1995 and are validated in this version since 1995.

Preamble

In the practice of the therapeutic profession, all members of the EAP national associations, EAP member organisations, as well as EAP individual members, accept that the practice of psychotherapy requires responsibility in relation to their own persons, their psychotherapeutic tasks as well as towards clients who have entrusted themselves to a professional psychotherapist and with whom they have thus entered a special relationship. EAP member organisations are responsible for concerning themselves with ethical questions. This is applicable to trainers, members and trainees of these organisations.

The ethical guidelines of the national organisations serve:
- to protect the patients/clients from unethical applications of psychotherapy by all its psychotherapists and training members.
- to set standards for its members.
- as a foundation for the settling of complaints.

1. Applicability

The following ethical guidelines are binding on all member organisations of EAP as well as individual members. EAP member institutions are obliged to have their own ethical guidelines that are compatible with those of the EAP.

2. The Psychotherapeutic Profession

The psychotherapeutic profession is a separate scientific profession. It deals with the diagnosing and comprehensive, knowledgeable and planned treatment of psychosocially and/or psychosomatically derived behavioural disturbances or states of suffering by means of scientific and psychotherapeutic methods. The psychotherapeutic process is based upon the interaction between one or more patients/clients and one or more psychotherapists with the aim of facilitating changes and further development.

The psychotherapeutic profession is characterised by its commitment to the responsible accomplishment of the aforementioned aims.

Psychotherapists are required to use their expertise while taking into account the individual's dignity and esteem, for the patient's/client's best interest. Psychotherapists must declare their professional status and training, as appropriate.

3. Professional Competence and Development

Psychotherapists are required to practise their profession in a competent and ethical manner. They are required to pay attention to research and developments in the scientific field of psychotherapy. To achieve this, practitioners need to ensure their on-going professional development. Psychotherapists should limit their practice to those areas and treatment methods where it can be proven that they have gained sufficient and certified knowledge and experience.

4. Confidentiality

Psychotherapists, as well as all support staff, are bound by principles of confidentiality regarding all information that has become known to them during their psychotherapeutic involvement/practice. The same applies to supervision.

5. Frame Issues

At the beginning of the psychotherapeutic treatment, psychotherapists are required to make the patient/client aware of their rights with special emphasis on the following:

* *The psychotherapeutic method employed (if appropriate and adequate to the process of the psychotherapeutic treatment) and the conditions (including the termination policy).

* *Extent and probable duration of the psychotherapeutic treatment.

* *Financial terms of the treatment (approximate fees, insurance claims, payment for missed sessions, etc.)

* *Confidentiality.

* *Complaints procedure.

The patient/client should be given the opportunity to decide whether they wish to enter psychotherapy and if so, with whom.

Psychotherapists are required to act responsibly, especially given the special nature of the psychotherapeutic relationship which is built on trust and a certain degree of dependency. Abuse and breach of trust is defined as psychotherapists' neglect of their professional responsibilities in relation to the patient/client in order to satisfy their own personal interests, be they sexual, emotional, social or financial. Any form of misuse is an offence against professional psychotherapeutic guidelines. The responsibility for this lies solely with the psychotherapist. Failure of responsibility in dealing with the trust and dependency relationship in psychotherapy is a serious error of treatment.

6. Factual/Objective and True Information

Information given to patients/clients must be factual/objective and true. Any blatant or misleading advertising is impermissible. Examples of this form of misleading and impermissible advertising could be: insupportable promises of healing or the quoting of many different types of psychotherapeutic methods (psychotherapeutic training begun without completion) which might give the impression of a more comprehensive or broader psychotherapeutic training than is the actual case.

7. Professional Relations with Colleagues

Psychotherapists, where necessary, are required to work interdisciplinarily with representatives of other professions for the well-being of the patient/client.

8. Ethical Guidelines for Training

The aforementioned ethical guidelines are also to be applied to the relationship between trainer and trainee, as appropriate.

9. Contribution to the Health Sector

As regards their social responsibility, psychotherapists are encouraged to make a contribution to the maintenance and creation of living conditions which will enhance, maintain and restore psychological health, and generally help further the maturity and development of people.

10. Psychotherapy Research

In the interest of the scientific-theoretical development of psychotherapy as well as psychotherapy outcome research, psychotherapists should participate in appropriate research projects. Psychotherapeutic research, as well as psychotherapy publications, are subject to the above ethical guidelines. The interests of the patients/clients are paramount.

11. Infringement of Ethical Guidelines

Each member organisation must have appropriate complaint and appeal procedures.

12. Duties of the National EAP Organisations

National organisations must require their practitioners to abide by codes of ethics that are compatible with EAP guidelines.

PART I

A National Register
of Psychotherapists in Ireland

ALDERDICE, John
ANDREWS, Paul
ARNOLD, Mavis
ARTHURS, Mary
AYLWIN, Susan

BAIRD, Jane
BANNON, John
BARRY, Kathleen
BARRY, Kay
BARRY, Myra
BAYLY, Kathrin
BELTON, Mary W.
BENSON, Jarlath F.
BERGIN, Alexander
BERMINGHAM, Paula
BOLAND, Emille
BONFIELD, Dymphna
BOROSON, Martin
BOURKE, Carmel
BOYLE, Martin
BOYNE, Edward
BREEN, Noreen
BREEN, Tom
BREHONY, Rita
BRENNAN, Mairtine
BRIGHT, Jill
BROPHY, John

BROWN, Essie
BROWN, Larry
BUCKLEY, Marguerite
BUCKLEY, Triona
BURSTALL, Taru
BUTCHER, Gerard
BUTLER, Goretti
BUTLER, Maggie
BYRNE, Carmel
BYRNE, Gerard
BYRNE, Kathleen
BYRNE, Mary
BYRNE, Nollaig
BYRNE, Padraic
BYRNE, Pat
BYRNE, Ruth

CADWELL, Nuala
CAHILL, Michelle
CALLANAN, Fiodhna
CALLANAN, William
CAMPBELL, Carmel
CANAVAN, Mary
CARBERRY, Brian
CARPENTER, Anne
CARR, Alan
CARROLL, Anna
CARROLL, Patricia

CARTON, Simone
CASEY, Grainne
CASSERLY, Felicity
CHILDERS, Nessa
CHOISEUL, Anne M.
CLAFFEY, Elaine
CLANCY, Mary
CLARKE, Margaret
CLARKE, Michele
COGHLAN, Helena
COLEMAN, Padraig
COLGAN, Patrick J.
COLLEARY, Maura
COLLINS, Deirdre
COLLINS, Geraldine
COLLINS, Ines
COLLINS, Mary
COLLINS-SMYTH, Margaret
COMERFORD, Anne
CONAGHAN, Mary
CONNEELY, Caitlin
CONNOLLY, Brendan
CONNOLLY, Brendan M.
CONNOLLY, Margaret
CONROY, Kay
CORKERY, Anne
COSTELLO, Margaret
COX CAMERON, Olga
COX, Ann
CUNNINGHAM, Kathy
CUNNINGHAM, Nora
CURTIN, Geraldine

DALY, Margaret
DALY, Martin
DALY, Martin J.
DAVEY, Damien

DE BURCA, Bairbe
DE JONGH, Corry
DE LACY, Mara
DEENY, Peggy
DEERY, Pat
DELMONTE, Michael M.
DENENY, Mary
DENNEHY, Noreen
DEVLIN, Fiona
DEVLIN, Teresa
DILLON, Kathleen
DOHERTY, Myra
DONNELLY, Pat
DONOGHUE, Mary
DONOHOE, Eugene
DONOHOE, Mary
DORR, Frank
DOWD, Teresa
DOWLING, Brenda
DOYLE, Mary
DOYLE, Rosaleen
DOYLE, Sherry
DRISCOLL, Angela
DRISCOLL, Zelie
DU LAING, Annemie
DUFFY, Kathleen
DUFFY, Martin
DUFFY, Mary
DUGGAN, Colman
DUGGAN, Noel
DULLAGHAN, Elizabeth
    (Lillie)
DUNNE, Ann Maria
DUNNE, Patricia
DWYER, Frankie-Ann

EGAN, Barbara
ELLIS, Mary

FADDEN, Rosaleen
FAHY, Michael
FAY, Joe
FERRITER, Kay
FINGLETON, May
FINLAYSON, Douglas
FINN, Monica Patricia
FINNEGAN, Leo J.
FITZGERALD, Barbara
FITZGERALD, Michael
FLEMING HOGAN
    Bernie
FLEMING, Pearl
FLYNN, Deirdre
FLYNN, Stephen
FOGARTY, Geraldine M.
FOLEY, Robert
FORBES, Jean
FORDE, Angela
FORREST, Mary
FOX, Michael
FOY, Emma
FRASER, Teresa
FRAWLEY, Angela
FRAWLEY, Michael
FRENCH, Gerry
FULTON, Linda

GAFFNEY, Delia
GALLIGAN, Patricia
GARLAND, Clive
GILL, Anne
GILL, Margaret
GILLILAND, Kay P.

GILMARTIN, Helen
GLEESON, Betty
GORDON, Evelyn
GRIEVE, Karin
GRIMLEY, Carmel
GRINDLEY, Geraldine M.
GROSSMAN FREYNE, Gail
GROVER, Mary
GUNNE, David
GUNNE, Dorothy

HAGAN, Patricia
HAMILL, Carmel
HARGIN, Mary Rose
HARRINGTON, Eileen
HAUGHTON, Helen
HAYES, Fran
HEALY, Daniel Christopher
HEALY, Donal
HEFFERNAN, Michael
HEGAN, Laurence
HEGARTY, Donal
HEGARTY, Owen
HEGARTY, Tony
HERLIHY, Marie.
HESKIN, Christina
HILL, Rosemary
HIRST, Iain J.
HOLLAND, Mary
HONNAY, Emiel
HORNER, Carol
HOULIHAN, Tom
HOWARD, Leslie
HOWLETT, Brian
HUGHES, Maria
HUMPHREYS, Vincent
HUNTER, Alison I.

JACKSON, Caitriona
JEBB, Winston
JENNINGS, Norman
JONES, Coleen
JONES, Helen
JOYCE, Nora
JUDGE, Jimmy
JUTHAN, Kay

KAVANAGH, Ann
KAY, Sarah
KEANE, Verena
KEARNEY, Philip
KEARNEY, Ruth
KEELAN, Annette
KEENAN, Marie
KEHOE, Helen
KEIGHER, Marian
KELLEHER, Kathleen
KELLIHER, Anne
KENNEDY, Jo
KENNY, Vincent
KIERNAN, Donal
KILCOYNE, Phyllis
KILGALLEN, Aideen
KILLORAN-GANNON,
    Sheila
KING, Margaret
KIRK, Geraldine
KOHNSTAMM, Barbara
KRZECZUNOWICZ,
    Sarah E. (Kay)

LALOR, Mary
LEE, Mary
LESLIE, Frank
LEWIS, Maeve

LIDDY, Rosemary
LINDEN, Mairead
LINDSAY, John
LINDSAY, Susan
LINNANE, Paul
LOGAN, Paddy
LONERGAN, Mary-Anna
LOUGHLIN, Paula
LUCEY, Joe
LYNCH, Catherine
LYNCH, Eileen

MAC GUINNESS, Irene
MAC NEILL, Sile
MACNAMARA, Vincent
MADDEN, Joan
MAGEE, David Louis
MAGENIS, Maire
MAGUIRE, Marie
MAGUIRE, Una
MAHER, Ann
MAHER, Bonnie
MAHER, Pascal
MANDOS, Koos
MANNION WALSHE,
    Deirdre
MARTIN, Maeve
MARTIN, Ray
MASTERSON, Ingrid
MATHEWS, Peter
MC ADAM, Frank
MC ALEER, Jennifer
MC CABE, Nancy
MC CARRICK, Tom
MC CARTHY, Aine
MC CARTHY, Anne
MC CARTHY, Dan

MC CARTHY, Eunice
MC CARTHY, Imelda
MC CARTHY, Rita
MC CARTHY, Ros
MC CASHIN, Dolores
MC COURT, Ann
MC COURT, Marie
MC CULLY, Maria
MC DONNELL, Patricia
MC FADDEN, Hugh
MC GEE, Annette
MC GEE, Breda
MC GLYNN, James
MC GLYNN, Peter
MC GOLDRICK, Mary
MC GRATH, Terri
MC GROARY-MEEHAN,
    Maureen
MC HALE, Edmund
MC HUGH, Charles
MC KEE, Maud
MC LEAVEY, Bernadette
MC LOONE, Anne
MC LOUGHLIN, Sarah
MC MANUS, Libby
MC MORROW, Mary
MC QUAID, Margaret
MEAGHER, Kathleen A.
MEEK, Pauline
MELVIN PERREM, Breda
MELVIN PERREM, Joan
MOHALLY, Derry
MOLEY, Patrick
MONAGHAN, Ann
MONAGHAN, Theresa
MONGEY, Sile

MOONEY MC GLOIN,
    Catherine
MOONEY, Alan A.
MOORE, Lucy
MORRISON, Anne
MOUNTAIN, Jane
MOYLAN, Bernadette
MULHERE, Jacinta
MULHOLLAND,
    Marie Therese
MULLER, Elisabeth
MURNANE, Eilis
MURPHY ROCHE, Freda
MURPHY, Ann C.
MURPHY, Brendan
MURPHY, David
MURPHY, Ger
MURPHY, John
MURPHY, Margaret
MURPHY, Mary
MURRAY, Claire
MURRAY, Denis
MURRAY, Janet
MURRAY, Marie
MYERS, Gerry

NANNERY, Teresa
NAUGHTON, Anne Marie
NEARY, Nora
NEVIN, Peter
NEWMAN, Josephine
NÍ CHONAOLA, Mairead
NÍ GHALLCHOBHAIR,
    Maighread
NÍ NUALLÁIN, Mairin
NÍ UALLACHÁIN, Meabh
NOLAN, Bernadette

NOLAN, Declan
NOLAN, Inger
NOLAN, Maeve
NOLAN, Patrick

O'BRIEN, David
O'BRIEN, Gay
O'BRIEN, Jim
O'BRIEN, Tom
O'BRIEN, Valerie
O'CONNOR, Colm J.
O'CONNOR, Elizabeth
O'CONNOR, Karen E.
O'CONNOR, Marika
O'CONNOR, Mary Rose
O'DALAIGH, Liam
O'DEA, Catherine
O'DEA, Eileen
O'DOHERTY, Colm
O'DONNELL, Godfrey
O'DONNELL, Ruth
O'DONOGHUE, Eilis
O'DONOGHUE, Jim
O'DONOGHUE, Paul
O'DONOVAN, Joan
O'DONOVAN, Mairin
O'DONOVAN, Margot
O'DOWD, Maura
O'DUFFY, Ann
O'DWYER, Mary
O'FLAHERTY, Anne
O'GRADY, Ethna
O'HALLORAN, Mary
O'HALLORAN, Mike
O'HANLON, Judy
O'HARA, Carmel
O'LEARY, Eleanor

O'MAHONY, Catherine
O'MAHONY, Eileen
O'MAHONY, Hank
O'MAHONY, Judy
O'MALLEY, Grace
O'MALLEY-DUNLOP,
    Ellen
O'NEILL, Ann
O'NEILL, Breege
O'NEILL, Deborah
O'NEILL, Elizabeth
O'NEILL, Julia
O'NEILL, Mary
O'NEILL, Nora
O'REILLY, Anne
O'REILLY, Joseph
O'REILLY, Maureen
O'ROURKE, Darina
O'SCOLLAIN, Eibhlin
O'SHAUGHNESSY, Marie
O'SULLIVAN, Bernadette
O'SULLIVAN, Creina
O'SULLIVAN, Marych
O'SULLIVAN, Michelle
O'TOOLE, Muriel
OWENS, Conor

PARKS, Ann
PEAKIN, Anne
PHALAN, Sally
PORTER, Sheila
PRENDERVILLE, Mary
PRICE, Noleen
PRYLE, Fiona M.
PYLE, Mary

REIDY, Margaret

REYNOLDS, Mary
RICHARDSON, Anne
RICHARDSON, Colette
RIORDAN, Gillian
ROCHE, Declan
ROCHE, Sile
ROE, Liam
ROTHERY, Nuala
RUSSELL, Maura
RUTH MURRAY, Ann M.
RYAN, Anne
RYAN, Catherine
RYAN, David
RYAN, Derval
RYAN, Eamonn
RYAN, Mairead
RYAN, Teresa
RYAN, Toni

SAHAFI, Janet E.
SCULLY, Patricia
SCULLY, Rosaleen
SELL, Patrick
SHEEHAN, Bartley
SHEEHAN, Jim
SHEEHAN, Thomas
SHEILL, Mary
SHERIDAN, Anne
SHEILDS, Vivienne
SHORTEN, Karen Ilean
SKAR, Patricia
SKELTON, Ross
SMITH, Mary
SMITH, Ray
SMITH, Susan
SMYTH, Geraldine
SOMMERS, Olive

SPARROW, Bobbie
STAUNTON, Pauline
STEFANAZZI, Mary
STEIN, Bernard N.
STONE, William
SWAIN, Ronny
SWEENEY, Brion
SWEENEY, Delma
SWEENEY, Patrick

TANSEY, Louise
TIERNEY, Aileen
TIERNEY, Maggie
TIGHE, Jacinta
TONE, Yvonne
TROOP, Deborah
TYRRELL, Patricia M.

UNDERWOOD-QUINN,
    Nicola

VAN DOORSLAER, Mia
VAN HOUT, Els

WADE, Richard
WALL MURPHY, Maura
WALLACE, George
WALSH, Angela
WALSH, Mary-Paula
WALSHE, Siobhan
WALSHE, Tony
WARD, Mary B.
WARD, Shirley A.
WARDEN, Norman
WATSON, Patricia
WEATHERILL, Rob
WHITE, Joan
WIECZOVEK-DEERING,
    Dorit

WILLIAMS, Jane
WOODS, Jean
WRAY, Andrew
WRIXON GOGGIN, Pauline
WYLIE-WARREN, Frances

YOUNG, Anne
YOUNG, Sheilagh

PART II

Approaches to Psychotherapy

Cognitive-Behavioural Psychotherapy (CBT)

The philosophical underpinning of this approach is that a person learns to act and think in certain ways as a result of their experiences and their perceptions of those experiences. This learning is a life-long process. Usually what we learn is adaptive and functional – we learn to become active participants in our lives, our society and our culture. However, occasionally we learn ways of thinking, feeling or behaving which hinder us in our development and prevent us from achieving our potential. Sometimes a single event such as being bitten by a dog, or a car crash, will have major repercussions; or, more often, experiences which go over a longer period of time, e.g. being bullied or being unemployed can affect us emotionally in the long term. Such negative experiences and responses to them can lead us to develop low self-esteem, unhappiness, bitterness, anxiety, passivity, aggression, perfectionism and so on. These, in turn, colour the way we perceive new experiences and at worst, if unchecked, can lead to such disorders as clinical depression, eating disorders, obsessive-compulsive disorder and panic disorder.

Clients present with a variety of different problems from a wide span of human experiences. Clients with a learning disability are helped to play a full part in society by extra teaching for the individual through a process of behaviour analysis. Each individual has the same rights and needs as everyone else in society. These clients' needs can be compounded due to

APPROACHES

physical disabilities, behavioural problems or communication deficits. Methods need to be used consistently within a particular context, by all of those involved, including the carer of the client who may have their own needs on a practical and emotional level. This approach examines people's behaviours in their living environment. It identifies the function challenging behaviour, services the individual, the source of the behaviour and its maintenance.

Clients experiencing stress and anxiety with marked avoidance behaviour (behaviour which postpones an anxiety evoking event and can lead to handicaps in every day life) can change their way of acting, e.g. become more outgoing and combat their fears with the help of individualised tailored Behaviour Therapy programmes.

They may have to confront repeatedly what they fear, e.g., contamination fear where the sufferer avoids certain perceived contaminated objects, progressing from the least feared object to the most feared. Personal accountability is the key to the client overcoming their problem. Motivation to complete home-work assignments and record progress between sessions, facilitates the carry-over into their daily lives of the skills and insights achieved by the client during therapy. This intervention and the willingness to explore new coping strategies are the ingredients for success.

Whereas in the past, Behaviour Therapy dealt only with what was observable, i.e. actions and behaviours, assuming rightly that once these were changed, thoughts and feelings would change to match the new behaviours. The cognitive therapists postulated that people can achieve change by working directly on their own patterns of thinking. Just as we may have, through our life experiences, learnt distorted patterns of thought (patterns which hinder rather than help), so can we learn new, helpful and functional thought patterns. The way we think impacts on every aspect of our lives, from hopefulness regarding the future, to personal relationships, to how we see ourselves and everything in between.

Cognitive and behavioural interventions overlap in their shared purpose of loosening the hold a particular negative belief has on the client and engaging him in a re-evaluation of his perceptions and assumptions.

The progress of the therapy is interactive. Its axis is in a relationship between the client and the therapist. The therapist uses a systematic framework that recognises the client as an individual and his/her need to be a participant in the solution to their own problems. People who experience interpersonal difficulties can benefit from group work using the key characteristics of the cognitive behavioural approach:

* assessment/analysis of the problem
* creating a therapeutic alliance
* agreed therapy goals and targets
* regular measurement and evaluation of progress towards targets.

Assessment is individual for each client. It involves detailed questioning and the use of psychological questionnaires to enable the client and therapist to define accurately the problem and set the goals of treatment. Cognitive-behavioural psychotherapy concentrates on the present – how we are now. It is practical and pragmatic, a collaborative effort by the therapist and client working together, rather like an investigative team; and is based on sound empirical findings. The aim of therapy is to provide the client with knowledge and techniques which he/she can use now and in the future, in effect, making the therapist redundant. Therapy is time limited and can be individual, family or group. Group treatment includes:

Assertiveness, Stress Management, Anger Management and Social Skills Training. Each client is given a detailed account of treatment options and their consent is sought before embarking on therapy. Registered practitioners adhere to a code of ethics, and are committed to research and the development of theory within this sphere.

Overall, practitioners use the developing pool of knowledge in this field to resolve problems of living for any person, irrespective of intelligence or insight.

Contact address: CBT, c/o Mary Reynolds,
St Vincent's Centre, Navan Road,
Dublin 7. Telephone: (01) 8383234

List of Practitioners

For addresses and telephone numbers, please refer to the Directory section.

BARRY, Kathleen
BUTCHER, Gerard
CLANCY, Mary
DEVLIN, Teresa
DOHERTY, Myra
FLEMING HOGAN, Bernie
MATHEWS, Peter
MC ADAM, Frank
MC FADDEN, Hugh
MC GLYNN, James
MC GLYNN, Peter

MC GOLDRICK, Mary
MC GROARY-MEEHAN, Maureen
MC HUGH, Charles
MOONEY MC GLOIN, Catherine
MULHERE, Jacinta
REYNOLDS, Mary
RYAN, Mairead
TONE, Yvonne

APPROACHES

Family Therapy (FTAI)

What is special about Family Therapy?

Family Therapy is the most popularly recognised descriptive title for a body of practice and theory which continues to evolve and to grow at an extraordinary rate. Originally, the approach was distinguished by the practice of including entire families in the therapy process rather than an individual client. This practice continues, but is not a necessary aspect of the approach. The principle which informed Family Therapy from the time of its inception in the 1950s has been to transcend simple cause and effect explanations which located deficits within the individual, and to include those aspects of the client's context in the therapy process which will enable them to manage, resolve or better understand their difficulty. It is this ecological view which attends to the interconnectedness of people, of beliefs and of all things, which characterises Family Therapy rather than the number of people sitting in the therapy room.

How do Family Therapists view problems and reality?

Many Family Therapists seek to engage the clients in a collaborative exploration of their presenting dilemma, focusing on the beliefs, and the interactions which maintain the difficulty or which prevent its resolution. By better understanding the interconnectedness of the biological, the social and the psychological dimensions of the problem, choices are intro-

duced, conflicts are transcended and new patterns of understanding are generated. Problems are frequently unwittingly
created by our well intentioned attempts to prevent difficulty.

A significant part of each one's experience is the beliefs, the
language, the stories and values which constitute our life experience. We are not only born into a material and physical
reality, but also into a multilayered complex weave of beliefs
and behaviours, which for most of us are, initially at least, of a
family nature. This strongly influences our developing 'reality'.
This reality is to us as water is to fish. In this context we grad-
ually learn to live in the world with greater autonomy, if all
goes well for us. We are born into the world totally dependent
on one or more caring adults, and if the constitutional and
contextual aspects of our lives are good enough, we learn to
operate more independently and to exercise choice in our
lives more effectively. This requires an appreciation of the in-
terdependence of our lives, of the world in which we live, and
the limits and possibilities which it contains. We constantly
explore the limits and possibilities of relying on previous
learning and exploring new ways and new beliefs. We may be
strongly influenced to find ways of being which contrast with
some of our significant life experiences, or we may repeat our
experiences, often with the assumption that this is how the
world is, and how everyone should be. When two or more
people live in close proximity, we can expect that differences,
and inevitably conflicts, will ensue. This is part of the rich weave
of our lives which continue to challenge us and to teach us.

Sometimes, our adult lives may be thrown into inner turmoil,
we may experience self-doubts, destructive feelings or immob-
ilising depression or anxiety. These disturbing experiences
may be triggered by what would be relatively small or man-
ageable difficulties for others, and even for ourselves in some-
what different circumstances. Such problems are frequently

APPROACHES

related to early life and usually early family aspects of our lives. Our difficulty trusting others, exercising choice or living with an adequate level of autonomy may be related to not having had sufficiently secure, loving or affirming experiences in our early family relationships. More recent traumas, abuse, oppression or unresolved conflict may also contribute to distressing inner feelings, which can be successfully resolved in Family Therapy. This healing, though a sometimes difficult and invariably challenging process, can enable us to make sense of our pain, doubts or confusion, to break through the log-jam and to proceed with living our lives more fully and negotiating life's transitions more successfully.

What do Family Therapists do?

Family Therapists universally employ the most inclusive frame with which to understand their clients, including early family experiences, and the beliefs, language and ways of behaving and relating which the client and those relevant to their problem or dilemma use. That confusing web, in which we remain engaged, and which influences and affects us as we struggle to extricate ourselves or to manage, to control or to change it, is the canvas upon which we work with clients. However, there are many different ways of engaging in this process. Some Family Therapists put most emphasis on exploring the beliefs, some the language and stories, and some the repeating behaviour patterns, the attempted solutions and others the exceptions, those experiences which work for the client, their successful solutions.

How many attend Family Therapy together?

The extent to which Family Therapists will emphasise including others in the process also varies. With relationship problems, we usually prefer to include the main participants. It is not uncommon for parents to successfully attend a series of consultations regarding one of their children, without the child being present. Extended family members may be invited or partners or others who are significantly involved in the client's life and difficulty. It is also common for individuals to attend alone, when the focus will include the significant relationships of their lives as the context of their emotional and psychological realities. Agreeing who will attend is usually an integral part of the exploratory process.

Some Family Therapists may also apply their systemic perspective to organisations such as schools, voluntary agencies, businesses and especially to family businesses. Consultation can help organisations to resolve intra organisations relationship problems and to address and to improve procedures and practices which influence their relationship with their consumers. The systemic consultant's focus will, again, include the context of the problem and can result in appreciating and fine tuning the ways in which the organisation responds to internal change and the range of changing external needs. The organisation, as the individual, can benefit by developing capacities of self-direction and responsivity.

Contact address: The Secretary, FTAI, 17, Dame Court, Dublin 2. Telephone: (01) 6794055

List of Practitioners

For addresses and telephone numbers, please refer to the Directory section.

BANNON, John	BYRNE, Padraic
BARRY, Myra	BYRNE, Pat
BAYLY, Kathrin	CADWELL, Nuala
BELTON, Mary W.	CALLANAN, William
BOURKE, Carmel	CARBERRY, Brian
BROPHY, John	CARR, Alan
BUCKLEY, Marguerite	CARROLL, Patricia
BUTLER, Goretti	CARTON, Simone
BYRNE, Mary	CLARKE, Michele

APPROACHES

APPROACHES

COLLINS, Geraldine
COLLINS, Ines
CONNEELY, Caitlin
CONNOLLY, Brendan
COSTELLO, Margaret
DALY, Martin
DE JONGH, Corry
DE LACY, Mara
DENNEHY, Noreen
DONOHOE, Eugene
DRISCOLL, Zelie
DUFFY, Mary
DUGGAN, Colman
DU LAING, Annemie
FADDEN, Rosaleen
FAY, Joe
FINGLETON, May
FINN, Monica Patricia
FITZGERALD, Barbara
FRASER, Teresa
FULTON, Linda
GAFFNEY, Delia
GILL, Margaret
GILLILAND, Kay P.
GLEESON, Betty
GORDON, Evelyn
GROSSMAN FREYNE, Gail
GUNNE, Dorothy
HAUGHTON, Helen
HAYES, Fran
HEGARTY, Donal
HIRST, Iain J.
HOLLAND, Mary
HOULIHAN, Tom
HOWARD, Leslie
HUGHES, Maria

HUMPHREYS, Vincent
JEBB, Winston
JUTHAN, Kay
KEANE, Verena
KEARNEY, Philip
KEENAN, Marie
KEIGHER, Marian
KELLEHER, Kathleen
KENNEDY, Jo
KILCOYNE, Phyllis
KIRK, Geraldine
KOHNSTAMM, Barbara
LALOR, Mary
LEE, Mary
LESLIE, Frank
LINNANE, Paul
MAC GUINNESS, Irene
MADDEN, Joan
MAGENIS, Maire
MAHER, Pascal
MANDOS, Koos
MC ALEER, Jennifer
MC CARTHY, Imelda
MC CARTHY, Ros
MC GEE, Breda
MC GRATH, Terri
MC HALE, Edmund
MC LOONE, Anne
MC LOUGHLIN, Sarah
MC MANUS, Libby
MC MORROW, Mary
MEEK, Pauline
MOLEY, Patrick
MONAGHAN, Ann
MONAGHAN, Theresa
MOORE, Lucy

MORRISON, Anne
MULHOLLAND,
  Marie-Therese
MURNANE, Eilis
MURPHY, John P.
MURPHY, Mary
MURPHY ROCHE, Freda
MURRAY, Denis
MURRAY, Marie
NOLAN, Declan
NOLAN, Inger
O'BRIEN, Gay
O'BRIEN, Jim
O'BRIEN, Tom
O'BRIEN, Valerie
O'CONNOR, Colm J.
O'DALAIGH, Liam
O'DEA, Eileen
O'DONNELL, Ruth
O'DONOVAN, Mairin
O'GRADY, Ethna
O'HARA, Carmel
O'MAHONY, Eileen
O'MALLEY-DUNLOP, Ellen
O'NEILL, Breege
O'NEILL, Elizabeth
O'SCOLLAIN, Eibhlin

O'SHAUGHNESSY, Marie
O'SULLIVAN, Creina
PORTER, Sheila
PRYLE, Fiona M.
REIDY, Margaret
RICHARDSON, Anne
RICHARDSON, Colette
ROCHE, Declan
ROCHE, Sile
ROE, Liam
SCULLY, Patricia
SHEEHAN, Jim
SHEEHAN, Thomas
SHIELDS, Vivienne
SHERIDAN, Anne
SMITH, Susan
STEIN, Bernard N.
SWEENEY, Patrick
TIERNEY, Aileen
TYRRELL, Patricia M.
UNDERWOOD-QUINN,
  Nicola
WALL MURPHY, Maura
WALSH, Angela
WHITE, Joan
YOUNG, Sheilagh M.

Humanistic and Integrative Psychotherapy (IAHIP)

APPROACHES

Therapists from a Humanistic and Integrative perspective invite people to develop their awareness as to what prevents them from unfolding their own true nature in the inner and outer expressions of their life.

Historical Context

The Humanistic Psychology movement developed in the 1960s in America out of a need to counter-balance the strong idealogical schools of scientific positivistic behaviourism and Freudian psychoanalysis. Both these ideological approaches to the person excluded some of the most important questions that make the human being human; for example, choice, values, love, creativity, self-awareness and human potential.

Yalom[1] makes an interesting observation as to the two strands underpinning the study of the nature of the person at that time, in both the European and American context. He says,

> '...it is interesting to note that the field of Humanistic Psychology developed alongside the 1960s counter culture in America with its attendant social phenomena such as the free speech movement, the flower children, the drug culture, the human potentialists and the sexual revolution', whereas '... the underpinnings of the European tradition of existentialist enquiry into the nature of the person was different. The existentialist position focused instead on human limitations and the tragic dimensions of existence'.[1]

This was partly shaped out of the society and culture at that time which had had a relatively recent history of war and geographic and ethnic confinement.

In contrast, the human potential movement was 'bathed in a zeitgeist of expansiveness, optimism, limitless horizons and pragmatism'.[1] The European existentialist tradition focused on limits, on facing and taking into oneself the anxiety of uncertainty and non-being, whereas the Human Potential movement spoke less of limits and contingency than of development of potential, less of acceptance than of awareness, less of anxiety than of peak experiences and oceanic oneness, less of life meaning than of self-realization, less of apartness and basic isolation than of I-Thou encounter.

These two strands of thought emphasise the fact that any attempt to describe the person merely as a part needs to include the whole, and that the human story and nature of the person is always articulated within the wider social and cultural context of which that person is a part.

The Nature of Humanistic and Integrative Psychotherapy

Within the Humanistic and Integrative approach, some commonly held assumptions about the human person are as follows:

- *the individual is seen as a whole person living out their present level of integration through their body, feelings, mind, psyche and spirit.*

- *a person has responsibility for his/her life and for the choices they make.* People are responsible not only for their actions but for their failures to act. A metaphorical way to describe this is to reflect on a person inhabiting themselves, not so much as a concrete structure embedded in stone, but more like a web spun by the shaping of their inner and outer life, which can be spun again in any number of ways.

APPROACHES

- *Humanistic and Integrative psychotherapy is based on a phenomenological view of reality.* Its emphasis is on experience. Therapists within this perspective frequently engage active techniques to encourage the deepening of the therapeutic process. There is a movement away from the goal of understanding events towards the active exploration of experience.

- *The nature of the person is seen as dynamic.* The person is seen as unfolding in different stages. There is always a thrust towards wholeness and life, but sometimes along the way, at any one stage, an overwhelming failure or frustration can be experienced as anxiety, depression or even a vague sense of an unlived life. These experiences can impede the emergence of later stages or result in an uneven integration as the person develops. Within each stage, different structures of relating to life emerge. Later structures transcend but include earlier ones, so that a question a person poses as they begin therapy, may be rooted in or have an echo in their earlier shaping, but will always include a harmonious note of future possibilities.

  We stretch to where we need to stretch, and what a humanistic and integrative therapist does is to be continually present to the unfolding nature and quest of the person within the therapeutic setting.

The Nature of the Therapeutic Process

Humanistic and Integrative therapies have many broad and creative approaches to working with clients. The therapeutic relationship is seen as a meaningful contract between equals, and the aims of therapy may be as diverse as encouraging the self-healing capacities of the client, to an exploration of a client's concrete individual experience of anxiety and distress rooted in earlier relationships, to an encouragement of insight into repeating patterns of behaviour which might be preventing clients from leading fulfilling and satisfying lives.

The attitude and presence of the therapist is important. Yalom[2] speaks about the therapist entering into the client's experiential world and listening to the phenomena of that world without the pre-suppositions that distort understanding. Carl Rogers[3] focused on the importance of deep, attentive listening on the part of the therapist in promoting change.

Integrative Aspects

Practitioners in this field come from a range of perspectives on what it means to be a person. Some emphasise the body aspects, other the experiential feeling life and awareness of the person presenting, and others the wider contexts of meaning of which that person is a part.

The integrative approach emphasises the validity of a variety of approaches to the individual, and whilst remaining respectful to each approach, draws from many sources in the belief that no one approach has the whole truth.

Therapists are always guided by the respect and acceptance of the client as a whole person who has the potential to change, heal and grow.

Irish Association of Humanistic and Integrative Psychotherapy

The Irish Association of Humanistic and Integrative Psychotherapy was formed in 1992 as an association to represent Humanistic and Integrative psychotherapists in Ireland. In 1994, the I.A.H.I.P. became a company, limited by guarantee, and is one of the five psychotherapy sections of the Irish Council for Psychotherapy.

The aims of the I.A.H.I.P. are to set and maintain standards of training and practice, and to accredit suitably qualified

APPROACHES

practitioners of psychotherapy. Members adhere to a code of ethics and practice which includes a complaints procedure.

Contact address: The Secretary
IAHIP, 82 Upper George's Street,
Dun Laoghaire, Co Dublin
Telephone: (01) 2841665

Notes
1. Yalom, Irwin D., *Existential Psychotherapy*, (Basic Books Inc., New York 1980).

2. *op. cit.* page 17.

3. Rogers, C., *On becoming a Person*, (Constable 1961).
— *Client-Centred Therapy*, (Constable 1965).
Further descriptions of Carl Rogers' work is contained in: Kirschenbaum, H. and Henderson, V. (eds), *The Carl Rogers Reader*, (Constable 1990).

Further Reading:
Rowan, J., *The Reality Game*, (Routledge & Keegan Paul, London 1983).
— *Subpersonalities*, (Routledge, London, 1990).
— *Ordinary Ecstasy*, (2nd Edition, 1988).
— *Humanistic Psychology in Action*, (Routledge, London).
— *The Transpersonal Psychotherapy and Counselling*, (Routledge, London, 1993).

Perls, F, Hefferline, R & Goodman, P., *Gestalt Therapy*, (Souvenir Press 1974).

Boadella, D., *Biosynthesis* (Routlege & Keegan Paul, 1987).

Lowen, A., *The Language of the Body*, (First Earlier Books, 1971).

Keleman, Stanley., *Emotional Anatomy* (Berkley, CA: Center Press, 1985).

Assagioli, R., *Photosynthesis: A Manual of Principles and Techniques*, (Turnstone Books, 1980).

Wilber, K., *Eye to Eye: The Quest for a new Paradigm*, (Anchor Books, 1983).

Grof, S., *Beyond the Brain* (Suny, 1985).

Grof, S. & Grof,C., *The Stormy Search for the Self*, (Tarcher 1970).

Rowan J. & Dryden, W. (eds), *Innovative Therapy in Britain*, (Open University Press, Milton Keynes, 1988).

Boyne, E. (ed), *Psychotherapy in Ireland*, (Columba Press, Dublin).

List of Practitioners
For addresses and telephone numbers, please refer to the Directory section.

ARNOLD, Mavis
ARTHURS, Mary
AYLWIN, Susan
BERGIN, Alexander
BOLAND, Emille
BONFIELD, Dympna
BOYNE, Edward
BREHONY, Rita
BRENNAN, Mairtine
BROWNE, Larry
BURSTALL, Taru
BUTLER, Maggie
BYRNE, Carmel
BYRNE, Kathleen
BYRNE, Ruth
CALLANAN, Fiodhna
CAMPBELL, Carmel
CANAVAN, Mary
CLAFFEY, Elaine
CLARKE, Margaret
COLGAN, Patrick J.
COLLEARY, Maura
COLLINS, Deirdre
COLLINS-SMYTH, Margaret
CONAGHAN, Mary
CONNOLLY, Brendan M.
CONROY, Kay
CUNNINGHAM, Kathy
CUNNINGHAM, Nora
CURTIN, Gerardine
DE BURCA, Bairbre
DEERY, Pat
DENENY, Mary
DEVLIN, Fiona

DOYLE, Mary
DOYLE, Rosaleen
DRISCOLL, Angela
DUFFY, Kathleen
DUFFY, Martin
DUGGAN, Noel
DULLAGHAN, Elizabeth
(Lillie)
DUNNE, Ann Maria
DUNNE, Patricia
DWYER, Frankie-Ann
ELLIS, Mary
FERRITER, Kay
FINLAYSON, Douglas
FITZGERALD, Barbara
FLEMING, Pearl
FLYNN, Stephen
FOGARTY, Geraldine M.
FORDE, Angela
FOX, Michael
FOY, Emma
FRAWLEY, Angela
FRAWLEY, Michael
GILL, Anne
GILMARTIN, Helen
GRIMLEY, Carmel
GRINDLEY, Geraldine M.
HAGAN, Patricia
HAMILL, Carmel
HARRINGTON, Eileen
HEALY, Daniel Christopher
HEALY, Donal
HEGARTY, Owen
HERLIHY, Marie

HESKIN, Christina
HILL, Rosemary
HONNAY, Emiel
HORNER, Carol
HOWLETT, Brian
HUMPHREYS, Vincent
HUNTER, Alison I.
JACKSON, Caitriona
JONES, Coleen
JONES, Helen
JOYCE, Nora
JUDGE, Jimmy
KEHOE, Helen
KELLIHER, Anne
KIERNAN, Donal
KILGALLEN, Aideen
KILLORAN-GANNON,
  Sheila
KING, Margaret
KOHNSTAMM, Barbara
KRZECZUNOWICZ, Sarah E.
LEWIS, Maeve
LIDDY, Rosemary
LINDEN, Mairead
LINDSAY, John
LINDSAY, Susan
LOGAN, Paddy
LONERGAN, Mary-Anna
LOUGHLIN, Paula
LYNCH, Catherine
MACNAMARA, Vincent
MAC NEILL, Sile
MAGUIRE, Una
MAHER, Ann
MANNION WALSHE, Deirdre
MARTIN, Ray

MC CARTHY, Anne
MC CARTHY, Dan
MC CASHIN, Dolores
MC COURT, Ann
MC COURT, Marie
MC CULLY, Maria
MC LEAVEY, Bernadette
MC QUAID, Margaret
MEAGHER, Kathleen A.
MELVIN PERREM, Breda
MOHALLY, Derry
MOONEY, Alan A.
MOUNTAIN, Jane
MOYLAN, Bernadette
MULLER, Elisabeth
MURPHY, David
MURPHY, Ger
MURRAY, Claire
MYERS, Gerry
NANNERY, Teresa
NÍ CHONAOLA, Mairead
NÍ UALLACHÁIN, Meabh
NOLAN, Inger
NOLAN, Patrick
O'CONNOR, Karen E.
O'CONNOR, Marika
O'DEA, Catherine
O'DOHERTY, Colm
O'DONOGHUE, Eilis
O'DONOGHUE, Jim
O'DONOGHUE, Paul
O'DONOVAN, Joan
O'DONOVAN, Margot
O'DOWD, Maura
O'DUFFY, Ann
O'DWYER, Mary

APPROACHES

O'HALLORAN, Mary

O'HALLORAN, Mike

O'HANLON, Judy

O'LEARY, Eleanor

O'MAHONY, Hank

O'NEILL, Ann

O'NEILL, Deborah

O'NEILL, Julia

O'NEILL, Mary

O'NEILL, Nora

O'REILLY, Joseph

O'REILLY, Maureen

O'ROURKE, Darina

O'TOOLE, Muriel

PARKS, Ann

PEAKIN, Anne

PRENDERVILLE, Mary

RIORDAN, Gillian

ROTHERY, Nuala

RUTH-MURRAY, Ann M.

RYAN, Anne

RYAN, Catherine

RYAN, David

RYAN, Teresa

RYAN, Toni

SAHAFI, Janet E.

SELL, Patrick

SHEILL, Mary

SHORTEN, Karen Ilean

SMYTH, Geraldine

SPARROW, Bobbie

STEFANAZZI, Mary

STEIN, Bernard

STONE, William

SWEENEY, Brion

SWEENEY, Delma

TIERNEY, Maggie

TROOP, Deborah

VAN HOUT, Els

WALLACE, George

WALSH, Mary-Paula

WARD, Mary B.

WARD, Shirley A.

WARDEN, Norman

WATSON, Patricia

WOODS, Jean

WRIXON GOGGIN, Pauline

APPROACHES

Constructivist Psychotherapy (ICPA)

APPROACHES

When a person seeks psychotherapy, they have a story to tell. It may be a troubled, hurt or angry story of a life or a relationship now spoiled. For many, it is a story of distressing events which seem to work against a sense of well-being, self confidence, or effectiveness in life. Whatever its form, a therapist is presented with a story, often persuasive and gripping. Of course there are many ways of responding to clients' stories, and different schools of therapy emphasise and engage different aspects of the story. A therapist working from a Constructivist or allied school will, from the outset, realise that a story is more than just a report of a person's experience. They will realise that a story also acts to create, sustain or alter ways in which a client understands and relates to their life circumstances. The therapist will be looking to what kinds of action a particular story invites into a person's life. What kind of understanding and conduct are being engendered, facilitated, or sustained as a result of their particular story. Therapists trained in this School of Psychotherapy will, in general, be concerned to find ways of inviting clients to attend to the manner in which their accounts, those of others, and that of the community in general, act as constraints to more co-operative personal engagements. The emphasis on an invitational approach to ways of making sense of experience is perhaps the clearest hallmark of Constructivist and related schools of therapy.

Expertise in objectivity is relinquished in favour of an invita tional exploration of possible ways of accounting and relating to circumstances. Therapists will generally be open to work with individuals, couples, families or wider groups.

For those with an academic or technical interest, some prominent key figures upon which this school of therapy intellectually, historically draws are, Gregory Bateson, George Kelly, David Smail, Miller Mair, W. Barrett Pearce, and Ken Gergen. Locally, key contributors have been Vincent Kenny and Bernadette O'Sullivan.

Some recommended reading would include:

Fay Fransella, *George Kelly*, (Sage Publications, London 1995)

Miller Mair, *Between Psychology and Psychotherapy: A Poetics of Experience*, (Routledge, London 1989)

Contact address: The Secretary, ICPA, 2, Dungar Terrace,
Northumberland Road, Dun Laoghaire,
Co Dublin. Telephone: (01) 2843336

List of Practitioners
For addresses and telephone numbers, please refer to the Directory section.

BAIRD, Jane	O'BRIEN, Gay
COLLINS, Mary	O'DONNELL, Godfrey
DAVEY, Damien	O'REILLY, Anne
GALLIGAN, Patricia	RUSSELL, Maura
GUNNE, Dorothy	SHEEHAN, Bartley
LUCEY, Joe	SWEENEY, Brion
MAGEE, David Louis	VAN DOORSLAER, Mia
MC KEE, Maud	WALSH, Mary-Paula

Psychoanalytic Psychotherapy

The three sub-divisions within this section are:
1. IFCAP
2. IFPP
3. IGAS

Child and Adolescent Psychoanalytic Psychotherapy (IFCAP)

Child and Adolescent Psychoanalytic Psychotherapy is a relatively new discipline in Ireland, although it has been practised widely in Europe and North America for fifty years. Most therapists working with children in Ireland have been trained under the auspices of the Irish Forum for Child and Adolescent Psychoanalytic Psychotherapy and Trinity College, Dublin. This therapy aims at helping children and adolescents learn a greater degree of self-understanding in the setting of a secure therapeutic relationship. Children are helped to learn, not only self awareness, but also how their pattern of relationships has been formed and how this may influence present experiences. Children in therapy are also afforded the opportunity to experience a new type of relationship in a safe, therapeutic setting. Such therapy can happen through a mixture of talk, play and activity.

Contact address: The Secretary, IFCAP,
13, Stradbrook Lawn,
Blackrock, Co Dublin
Telephone: (01) 2806623

The Irish Forum for Psychoanalytic Psychotherapy (IFPP)

Members of the Irish Forum for Psychoanalytic Psychotherapy (IFPP) are professional psychotherapists who come from the different schools of psychoanalytic thought which originated with Freud in the late 19th century. Psychoanalytic Psychotherapy involves uncovering unconscious conflicts and causes of distress and elucidating desires both conscious and unconscious by means of free association, exploration of dream material, feelings and memories. The working through of this material brings alive both the past and the present.

The Irish Forum for Psychoanalytic Psychotherapy was founded in 1986 with the aim of providing coherent focus for those people throughout the island with a serious interest in the advancement of the study and practice of psychoanalytic psychotherapy, which remains central to the organisation today. All full members of the IFPP have fulfilled training requirements which are in line with colleagues in the rest of Europe.

Contact address: The Secretary, IFPP, 13, Cherry Court, Cherrywood, Loughlinstown, Co Dublin. Telephone: (01) 2823582

Group Analysis (IGAS)

Group Analysis is a method of group psychotherapy which was initiated in 1940 in England by the late Dr. S. H. Foulkes and has since been refined and developed by an ever widening circle of associates of practitioners, both in England and abroad.

Irish Context

In 1987, the Institute of Group Analysis London, in association with the School of Psychotherapy St Vincent's Hospital and University College Dublin, established the Group Analytic Psychotherapy Training in Ireland. The first Group

Analysts graduated in 1994 and at present, there are 60 trainees at varying stages in the training programme. In the Spring of 1996, the newly formed Irish Group Analytic Society ran its first Public Workshop in Dublin entitled 'Loss, Change and Creativity'. The workshop succeeded very well in its aim, which offered an opportunity for people working with Groups, and for individuals, to gain an experience of Group Analysis through working with this particular theme which has such important personal and social implications for Ireland at the present time.

What is Group Analysis?

Group Analysis is primarily a method of group psychotherapy which combines psychoanalytic insights with an understanding of social and interpersonal factors. It focuses on the relationship between the individual and the group in order to strengthen the development of both. The ultimate aim is to achieve the integration of the individual in his or her communal network, which is the hallmark of a healthy society. Its orientation is analytic, deriving from the principles of psychoanalysis, but differing from psychoanalysis in the light of certain important concepts that have been arrived at by considering the individual member in the context of the group as a whole. Group Analysis focuses on the dynamics within the group between all its members, including the therapist.

How does it work?

In practice, the small analytic group consists of not more than eight members and the analyst. Members will not be known to each other before joining the group, and social contact outside the group is discouraged. The groups will contain both men and women and members will join for a variety of reasons. Confidentiality is of the utmost importance. The group will usually meet once or twice a week at the same time and in the same place for a duration of one and a half hours, and all the business of the group is conducted and contained within this time. This type of group will continue to exist for many years, and the membership will change as the individuals are ready to leave and new members join. The analyst will assess each individual member, and there will be a short period of preparation, before joining the group. The process of change is a slow process and for a member to get maximum benefit from the group therapeutic situation, members would stay for about two years minimum. Most analysts work on a sliding scale, and usually each session costs approximately £15.

Applied Group Analysis

Group Analytic Psychotherapy is also widely applied in the work setting with staff and with small and large working groups, and with psychological problems with children, adolescents, couples and the elderly. Other areas of therapeutic application include: learning disabilities, psychosexual and psychosomatic problems, alcohol and drug dependence, eating, mood and personality disorders, psychosis and long-term mental illness. The three main groups in which group analytic psychotherapy is practised, are the small group (as described above), the medium group (more than 10 and less than 25) and the large group (more than 25 and upwards).

The Core Professions

The core professions of the Group Analysts include Psychiatrists, Psychologists, Social Workers, Nurses, Counsellors, Teachers, Clergy/Religious and Occupational Therapists. The Group Analysts work both in the Private and the Public Sectors.

Contact Address: The Secretary, IGAS, 52, Castlepark Rd, Sandycove, Co. Dublin.
Telephone: (01) 2857459

List of Practitioners

For addresses and telephone numbers, please refer to the Directory section.

IFCAP

ANDREWS, Paul
BREEN, Noreen
CASEY, Grainne
CONNOLLY, Margaret
DONNELLY, Pat
DOYLE, Sherry
FORBES, Jean
HARGIN, Mary Rose
MARTIN, Maeve
MURRAY, Janet
NEARY, Nora
NÍ GHALLCHOBHAIR,
    Maighread
O'FLAHERTY, Anne
O'SULLIVAN, Marych
OWENS, Conor
PHALAN, Sally
WIECZOVEK-DEERING,
    Dorit

IFPP

BOYLE, Martin
BRIGHT, Jill
CASSERLY, Felicity
CHILDERS, Nessa
COX, Ann
COX CAMERON, Olga
DALY, MARTIN J.
DELMONTE, Michael M.
DONOGHUE, Mary
FRENCH, Gerry
GLEESON, Betty
GRIEVE, Karen
GROVER, Mary
JENNINGS, Norman
KEARNEY, Ruth
MAHER, Bonnie
MASTERSON, Ingrid
MC CARRICK, Tom

MURPHY, Ann C.
MURPHY, Brendan
NÍ NUALLÁIN, Mairin
NOLAN, Maeve
NOLAN, Patrick
O'MAHONY, Catherine
O'MALLEY-DUNLOP, Ellen
O'SULLIVAN, Marych
PYLE, Mary
SKAR, Patricia
SKELTON, Ross
WYLIE-WARREN, Frances
YOUNG, Anne

IGAS

BENSON, Jarlath F.
BERMINGHAM, Paula
CHOISEUL, Anne M.
COGHLAN, Helena
DEENY, Peggy
DOWD, Teresa
FAHY, Michael
FINNEGAN, Leo J.
GARLAND, Clive
NÍ NUALLÁIN, Mairin
O'BRIEN, David
O'CONNOR, Elizabeth
O'MAHONY, Judy
O'MALLEY-DUNLOP, Ellen
PYLE, Mary
RYAN, Derval
SOMERS, Olive
SMITH, Ray

PART III

A Directory
of Psychotherapists in Ireland

ANDREWS, Paul
36 Lower Leeson Street,
Dublin 2.
Tel: 01-6767321
Therapy with people under 20.
IFCAP

ARNOLD, Mavis
Rosney Mews,
Albert Road,
Glenageary,
Co Dublin.
Tel: 01-2805575
Humanistic & integrative
IAHIP

ARTHURS, Mary
Dubhlinn Institute,
16 Prospect Road,
Glasnevin,
Dublin 9.
Tel: 01 - 8302358
Humanistic & integrative psychotherapist.
IAHIP

AYLWIN, Susan
Dept. of Applied Psychology,
University College,
Cork.
Tel: 021-902368/902410
Integrative
IAHIP

BAIRD, Jane
39 Old Kilmainham Village,
Bow Lane West,
Dublin 8.
Tel: 01-6708468
Work with individuals & couples on addiction, depression, relationship, sexual abuse, anxiety & panic disorders using broadly constructivist approach, art & dream work included.
ICPA

BANNON, John
St Fintan's Hospital,
Portlaoise,
Co Laois.
Tel: 0502 - 21364
Systemic - Eclectic
FTAI

BARRY, Kathleen
Mental Health Centre,
Markievicz House,
Barrack Street,
Sligo.
Tel: 071-55120
Cognitive behavioural
CBT

BARRY, Myra
Castleknock Child & Family Centre,
EHB,
Dublin 15
Tel: 01-8214385
Child, Systems, Grief
FTAI

DIRECTORY

BAYLY, Kathrin
29 College Park Way,
Dundrum, Dublin 16.
Tel: 01-2960803/086-8146929
Individual couples & family therapy.
Drug misuse.
FTAI

BELTON, Mary W.
Lucena Clinic,
Century Court,
100 George's Street,
Dun Laoghaire, Co Dublin.
Tel: 01-2885511
Family therapy.
FTAI

BENSON, Jarlath F.
Belfast Psychotherapy & Training Ctr.,
Office 22,
40 Victoria Square,
Belfast BT1 4QB.
Tel: 01232-242597
Group Analyst
IGAS

BERGIN, Alexander
6 Patrick Street,
Mountmellick, Co Laois.
Tel: 0502-24299
Psychosynthesis
IAHIP

BERMINGHAM, Paula
26 Fitzwilliam Square, Dublin 2.
Tel: 01- 4908315/6763036
Group Analysis
IGAS

BOLAND, Emille
206 Moyville,
Rathfarnham, Dublin 16.
Tel: 01-4945818
Integration of body, mind & spirit.
Eclectic.
IAHIP

BONFIELD, Dympna
181 Strand Rd.,
Sandymount, Dublin 4.
Tel: 01-2830593
Art psychotherapy.
IAHIP

BOURKE, Carmel
St Anne's Secondary School,
Tipperary Town,
Co Tipperary.
Tel: 062 - 51747
Bereavement, addictions, marital &
family therapy
FTAI

BOYLE, Martin
46A Village Green,
Tallaght,
Dublin 24.
Tel: 01-4621263
Psychoanalytic psychotherapy
IFPP

BOYNE, Edward
24 Clarinda Park East,
Dun Laoghaire, Co Dublin.
Tel: 01-2809178
Humanistic & integrative
IAHIP

BREEN, Noreen
CDVEC Psychological Service,
25 Temple Road,
Dartry, Dublin 6.
Tel: 01 -4971442
IFCAP

BREHONY, Rita
18 Glenard Ave,
Salthill, Galway.
Tel: 091-522648
Bio-dynamic,body oriented, humanistic
& integrative
IAHIP

BRENNAN, Mairtine
Douglas,
Cork.
Tel: 021-775875
Women, trauma, assertion, adult children of alcoholics.
IAHIP

BRIGHT, Jill
2 Alexandra Place,
Cork.
Tel: 021-507360
Jungian analyst
IFPP

BROPHY, John
Marino, Dublin 3.
Tel: 01-8338615
Marital & family therapy, sexual abuse therapy. (5yrs experience Rape Crisis Centre)
FTAI

BROWNE, Larry
Cork.
Tel: 021-963511
Holistic approach to psychotherapy & group work.
IAHIP

BUCKLEY, Marguerite
Pastoral Centre Arus de Brun,
Newtownsmith, Galway.
Tel: 091-565066
Bereavement counselling, individual/group, general grief, suicide, separation.
FTAI

BURSTALL, Taru
National Training College,
Beach Road, Sandymount,
Dublin 4.
Tel: 01-2057287
IAHIP

BUTCHER, Gerard
St John of God Hospital,
Stillorgan,
Co. Dublin.
Tel: 01-2881781 Ext. 242
Behavioural psychotherapist
CBT

BUTLER, Goretti
14 Baggot Road,
Navan Road,
Dublin 7.
Tel: 01-8686050
Family,couple & individual therapy
FTAI

BUTLER, Maggie
82 Upper George's Street,
Dun Laoghaire,
Co Dublin.
Tel: 087-607258
IAHIP

BYRNE, Carmel
'Amethyst',
28 Beechcourt,
Killiney,
Co Dublin.
Tel: 01-2850976
Eclectic, humanistic, pre & perinatal psychotherapist, primal integration & regression, infant & childbirth refacilitation.
IAHIP

BYRNE, Kathleen
Acorn Counselling,
Wellington Quay,
Drogheda, Co Louth.
Tel: 041-44277
Humanistic & integrative
IAHIP

BYRNE, Mary
7 Ben Edair Road,
Dublin 7.
Tel: 01-8382803
Family therapy
FTAI

BYRNE, Padraic
St Brigid's Hospital,
Ardee,
Co Louth.
Tel: 041-53264
Family therapist.
FTAI

BYRNE, Pat
Tralee General Hospital,
Tralee,
Co Kerry.
Tel: 066-26222
Family therapy
FTAI

BYRNE, Ruth
Coolagh,
Dungarvan,
Co Waterford.
Tel: 058-43057/42096
Client centred Gestalt therapist with individuals, couples, groups & supervision.
IAHIP

CADWELL, Nuala
Connect Associates,
Lonsdale House,
Avoca Avenue,
Blackrock,
Co Dublin.
Tel: 01-2884155
Systemic family therapy.
FTAI

CALLANAN, Fiodhna
148 Pearse Street,
Dublin 2.
Tel: 01-4592107
Humanistic & integrative
IAHIP

CALLANAN, William
Milltown Park,
Sandford Road,
Dublin 6.
Tel: 01-2698411
Marital & family therapy, analytical psychology
FTAI

CAMPBELL, Carmel
Institute of Creative Counselling &
Psychotherapy,
82 Upr. George's Street,
Dun Laoghaire, Co Dublin.
Tel: 01-2802523
Humanistic & integrative
IAHIP

CANAVAN, Mary
'Avalon', 8 Alma Park,
Monkstown Village,
Monkstown,
Co Dublin.
Tel: 01-2845208
Integrative psychotherapy with analytic experience & learning.
IAHIP

CARBERRY, Brian
Hampton Mental Health Centre,
Hampton Street,
Balbriggan,
Co Dublin.
Tel: 01-8413930/1
Family, couples & individual therapy.
FTAI

CARR, Alan
Clanwilliam Institute,
18 Clanwilliam Terrace,
Dublin 2.
Tel: 01-6761363/6762881
Family therapy.
FTAI

CARROLL, Patricia
Clanwilliam Institute,
Shankill, Co Dublin.
and
Newtownmountkennedy,
Co Wicklow.
Tel: 01-2873162/6761363
Family & marital therapist.
FTAI

CARTON, Simone
National Brain Injury Unit,
National Rehabilitation Hospital,
Rochestown Avenue,
Dun Laoghaire,
Co Dublin.
Tel: 01-2854777 Ext.326
Systemic therapy
FTAI

CASEY, Grainne
Arduna,
55 Clontarf Road,
Dublin 3.
Tel: 01-8332733
Child & adolescent psychotherapist.
IFCAP

CASSERLY, Felicity
Blackrock,
Co Dublin.
Tel: 01-2882286
Psychoanalytic
IFPP

CHILDERS, Nessa
14 Gledswood Avenue,
Clonskeagh,
Dublin 14.
Tel: 01-2697682
Psychoanalytic psychotherapy.
IFPP

CHOISEUL, Anne M.
St Vincent's Hospital,
Elm Park,
Dublin 4.
Tel: 01-2694533
Group analytic psychotherapy
IGAS

CLAFFEY, Elaine
4 Ashgrove Cottages,
Dundrum,
Dublin 14.
Tel: 01-2962115
Humanistic & integrative using a wide range of skills from bodywork to art & claywork.
IAHIP

CLANCY, Mary
Donegal Community Services,
East End House,
Donegal Town.
Tel: 073-21933
Behaviour psychotherapist
CBT

CLARKE, Margaret
23 Lwr. Albert Road,
Sandycove,
Co Dublin.
Tel: 01-2808989
Integrated psychotherapy incorporating psychoanalytic, body oriented & process oriented psychotherapy.
IAHIP

CLARKE, Michele
39 Westfield Road, Dublin 6W.
Tel: 01-4922209
Systems therapy, team work, residential child care.
FTAI

COGHLAN, Helena
41 Lower Baggot Street, Dublin 2.
Tel: 01-6609490
Group analytic psychotherapy.
IGAS

COLGAN, Patrick J.
Eckhart House,
19 Clyde Road, Dublin 4.
Tel: 01-6684687
Psychosynthesis
IAHIP

COLLEARY, Maura
Eckhart House,
19 Clyde Road, Dublin 4.
Tel: 01-2844256
Psychosynthesis
IAHIP

COLLINS, Deirdre
Kiltalown House, Blessington Rd.,
Tallaght, Dublin 24.
and
Aistear, 56 Percy Lane, Ballsbridge, D.4.
Tel: 01-4937394
Humanistic & integrative psychotherapy for individuals.
IAHIP

COLLINS, Geraldine
Health Centre,
Shannon,
Co Clare.
Tel: 061-362491 / 087-2393971
Systemic family therapy.
FTAI

COLLINS, Ines
Clanwilliam Institute,
18 Clanwilliam Terrace, Dublin 2.
Tel: 01-6762881/6761363
Family therapy.
FTAI

COLLINS, Mary
Rock Road Psychotherapy Centre,
110 Rock Road,
Booterstown, Co Dublin.
Tel: 01-2882749
Mind-body-spirit Holistic psychotherapy. Hakoni information, trainings & workshops organiser.
ICPA

COLLINS-SMYTH, Margaret
'Mignon',
Corbally Road,
Limerick.
Tel: 061-347506
Humanistic & integrative psychotherapy, individual & groupwork, supervision & training.
IAHIP

CONAGHAN, Mary
18 Casimir Road,
Harold's Cross,
Dublin 6W.
Tel: 01-4908883
Humanistic & integrative
IAHIP

CONNEELY, Caitlin
Caoineas,
The Glebe,
Tuam, Co Galway.
Short-term dynamic psychotherapy, family & systemic therapy.
FTAI

CONNOLLY, Brendan
Moore Abbey,
Monasterevin, Co Kildare.
Tel: 045-525327
The evolving individual in a social system (s).
FTAI

CONNOLLY, Brendan M.
7 Brookville Estate,
Glanmire, Co Cork.
Tel: 021-821774
Awareness therapy.
IAHIP

CONNOLLY, Margaret
24 Dornden Park, Booterstown, Co Dublin
and
Merrion Medical Centre,
Merrion Road, Dublin.
Tel: 01-2838441
Children & adolescents - post traumatic stress disorder - bereavement - brief psychotherapy.
IFCAP

CONROY, Kay
Turning Point,
23 Crofton Road,
Dun Laoghaire, Co Dublin.
Tel: 01-2801094
Psychospiritual, cancer/bereavement, long term/life threatening/terminal illnesses, marriage relationship/family mediation, supervision, sexual abuse, groups.
IAHIP

COSTELLO, Margaret
Child Psychiatric Team
Regional Child & Family Centre,
St Mary's, Dublin Road,
Drogheda, Co. Louth.
Tel: 041-30990/1
Family therapy.
FTAI

COX, Ann
Arduna Counselling &
Psychotherapy Centre,
55 Clontarf Road,
Dublin 3.
Tel: 01-8332733
Psychoanalytical psychotherapy with individuals.
IFPP

COX CAMERON, Olga
19 Belgrave Square,
Monkstown,
Co Dublin.
Tel: 01-2808868
Psychoanalyst
IFPP

CUNNINGHAM, Kathy
Tracht Beach,
Kinvara,
Galway.
Tel: 091-637192
Biodynamic & process oriented.
IAHIP

CUNNINGHAM, Nora
Dirreen, Athea,
Co Limerick.
Tel: 068-42232
Biodynamic & integrative psychotherapy.
IAHIP

CURTIN, Gerardine
Psychology Dept., NWHB,
Markievicz House,
Sligo.
Tel: 071-55132
Integrative psychotherapy, analytically based incorporating Gestalt & body oriented perspectives.
IAHIP

DALY, Martin
CUS, 89 Lr. Leeson Street,
Dublin 2.
Tl: 01-6762586/6619995
Systemic family therapy
FTAI

DALY, Martin J.
2 Church Lane,
Lr. Kilmacud Road, Co Dublin.
Tel: 01-2882257
Psychoanalysis
IFPP

DAVEY, Damien
5 St Enda's Drive,
Grange Road,
Rathfarnham, Dublin 14.
Tel: 01-4978476
Individual & relationship therapist.
ICPA

DE BURCA, Bairbre
Eckhart House,
Clyde Road, Dublin 4.
Tel: 01-6684687
Psychosynthesis
IAHIP

DEENY, Peggy
Mourneside Family Practice,
Strabane Co Tyrone BT82 9AF
and
Main Street, Stranorlar, Co Donegal.
Tel: 01504-351374 / 074-32746
Group analyst.
IGAS

DEERY, Pat
Dundalk Counselling Centre,
Oakdene, 3 Seatown Place,
Dundalk, Co Louth.
Tel: 042-38333
*Person-centred, eclectic, special interest
in adolescent therapy.*
IAHIP

DE JONGH, Corry
Clanwilliam Institute,
18 Clanwilliam Terrace,
Dublin 2.
Tel: 01-6761363/6762881
Couple & family therapy
FTAI

DE LACY, Mara
St Patrick's Hospital,
James' Street, Dublin 8.
Tel: 01-6775423
Addiction & the family; serious illness
FTAI

DELMONTE, Michael M.
St Patrick's Hospital,
James' Street, Dublin 8.
Tel: 01-6775423 (W) / 2804477 (H)
*Psychoanalytic psychotherapy & psycho-
dynamics*
IFPP & ICPA

DENENY, Mary
6 Francis Street,
Galway.
Tel: 088-624023
Biodynamic & integrative
IAHIP

DENNEHY, Noreen
Clanwilliam Institute,
18 Clanwilliam Terrace,
Grand Canal Quay, Dublin 2.
Tel: 01- 6761363/6762881
Couple & family therapist
FTAI

DEVLIN, Fiona
6, Sydney Place,
Wellington Road, Cork.
Tel: 021-507247
*Integrative psychotherapy - individuals,
couples & groups.*
IAHIP

DEVLIN, Teresa
Millbrae Surgery,
Millbrae, Carndonagh, Co Donegal.
Tel: 077-74644
Cognitive therapist dealing with children & adults.
CBT

DOHERTY, Myra
Day Centre,
The Rock,
Ballymote, Co Sligo.
Tel: 071-83002
Behavioural psychotherapy
CBT

DONNELLY, Pat
51 Sugarloaf Crescent,
Bray, Co Wicklow.
Tel: 01-2864053
Children & adolescents; bereavement children & adults.
IFCAP

DONOGHUE, Mary
59 Waterloo Lane, Dublin 4.
Tel: 01-2823582
Psychoanalytic psychotherapy
IFPP

DONOHOE, Eugene
Mater Child & Family Centre,
Ballymun Shopping Centre,
Dublin 11.
Tel: 01-8420319
Family therapist.
FTAI

DOWD, Teresa
St Camillus Unit,
St Vincent's Hospital,
Elm Park, Dublin 4.
Tel: 01-2094577
Group analyst.
IGAS

DOYLE, Mary
16 Salmon View Terrace,
Sunday's Well Avenue, Cork.
Tel: 021-301187
Humanistic & integrative.
IAHIP

DOYLE, Rosaleen
Eckhart House,
19 Clyde Road, Dublin 4.
Tel: 01-6684687
Psychosynthesis psychotherapist
IAHIP

DOYLE, Sherry
98 Lower Churchtown Road,
Dublin 14.
Tel: 01-2960918
Child & adolescent psychoanalytic psychotherapy
IFCAP

DRISCOLL, Angela
Front Garden Flat,
43 Alma Road,
Monkstown, Co Dublin.
Tel: 01-2843172
Integrated psychoanalytic,process oriented, body psychotherapy.
IAHIP

DRISCOLL, Zelie
44 Lr. Newcastle,
Galway.
Tel: 091-791087
Individual & marital therapy, addictions
FTAI

DUFFY, Kathleen
Westport Road,
Castlebar, Co Mayo.
Tel: 094-24206
Dreamwork/relationships, inner child work, creative visualisation, totem pole process.
IAHIP

DUFFY, Martin
Hawthorn Cottage,
Horseshoe Lane,
Allenstown,
Kells, Co Meath.
Tel: 046-49446
*All areas of humanistic, Jungian,
transpersonal approach, holotropic
breathwork, TM, Shamanic counselling.*
IAHIP

DUFFY, Mary
Glenmalure Day Hospital,
Milltown Road,
Dublin 6.
Tel: 01-2830388
Marital & family therapy.
FTAI

DUGGAN, Colman
Our Lady's Hospital for Sick Children,
Crumlin,
Dublin 12.
Tel: 01-4558220/1
Systemic & psychoanalytic therapy.
FTAI

DUGGAN, Noel
3, Greenview Heights,
Inishannagh Park,
Newcastle,
Galway.
Tel: 091-526126
Biodynamic, integrative & imagework.
IAHIP

DULLAGHAN, Elizabeth
(Lillie)
Dundalk Counselling Centre,
'Oakdene',
3 Seatown Place,
Dundalk, Co Louth.
Tel: 042-38333 (W) 042-33674 (H)
Humanistic & integrative.
IAHIP

DUNNE, Ann Maria
Chrysalis,
Donard,
Co Wicklow.
Tel: 045-404713
*Humanistic approach using Gestalt &
psychodrama to release emotions.*
IAHIP

DUNNE, Patricia
3 Seatown Place,
Dundalk, Co Louth.
Tel: 042-71976
*Humanistic, integrative, individual &
couples.*
IAHIP

DWYER, Frankie-Ann
9 Albany Road,
Ranelagh, Dublin 6.
Tel: 01-4973425
Integrative.
IAHIP

ELLIS, Mary
1 The Crescent,
Cobh, Co Cork.
Tel: 021-811679
Adults & children.
IAHIP

FADDEN, Rosaleen
Ionad Follain,
Myshall, Co Carlow.
Tel: 0503-57810
Family therapy & addiction counselling.
FTAI

FAHY, Michael
47 Woodfield,
Cappagh Road,
Barna, Galway.
Tel: 091-590350
Group analytic psychotherapy.
IGAS

FAY, Joe
Probation & Welfare Service,
Smithfield Chambers,
Smithfield,
Dublin 7.
Tel: 01-8733722
Marriage & family therapy.
FTAI

FERRITER, Kay
Dundrum Gestalt Centre,
Park House,
Upper Kilmacud Road,
Dublin 14.
Tel: 01-2962015
*Humanistic & Gestalt therapist working
with individuals, couples & groups.
Special interest issues of sexuality &
training.*
IAHIP

FINGLETON, May
Coote Street,
Portlaoise,
Co Laois.
Tel: 0502-27176/ 087-2310008
Family therapist.
FTAI

FINLAYSON, Douglas
2 Alexandra Place,
St Lukes,
Cork.
Tel: 021-500307
Integrative.
IAHIP

FINN, Monica
Eastern Health Board,
Glenmalure Day Hospital,
Milltown Road,
Dublin 6.
Tel: 01-2830388/98
Marital & family therapist.
FTAI

FINNEGAN, Leo J.
Human Development & Relations
Practice,
Glencar Scotch,
Letterkenny,
Co Donegal.
Tel: 074-26405
Analytic
IGAS

FITZGERALD, Barbara
Eckhart House,
19 Clyde Road,
Ballsbridge, Dublin 4.
Tel: 01-2894787
*Psychosynthesis, body movement, systemic
family therapy.*
IAHIP & FTAI

FLEMING, Pearl
4 Pembroke Cottages,
PYE Centre,
Dundrum,
Dublin 14.
Tel: 01-2962115
*Humanistic, integrative & addiction
counselling.*
IAHIP

FLEMING HOGAN, Bernie
Behaviour Psychotherapy Dept.,
The Annex,
St Brendan's Hospital,
North Circular Road,
Dublin 7.
Behavioural psychotherapy.
CBT

FLYNN, Stephen
SHB,
Neighbourhood Youth Project,
Mayfield, Cork.
Tel: 021-501674
Psychiatric patients.
IAHIP

DIRECTORY

FOGARTY, Geraldine M.
68 Indian Trail,
Toronto,
Ontario M6R 1Z9,
Canada.
Tel: 001-416 766 7495
Analytical psychotherapy
IAHIP

FORBES, Jean
Arduna Counselling & Psychotherapy
Centre,
55 Clontarf Road,
Dublin 3.
Tel: 01-8332733
Psychoanalytic psychotherapy
IFCAP

FORDE, Angela.
Knock Shrine,
Knock,
Co Mayo.
Tel: 094-88100
Gestalt, integrative.
IAHIP

FOX, Michael
12 Wainsfort Drive,
Terenure,
Dublin 6W.
Tel: 01-4906796
*Integrated approach - psychodynamic,
body centered & humanistic*
IAHIP

FOY, Emma
The Mews,
Summerhill House,
Marino Avenue West,
Killiney, Co Dublin.
Tel: 01-2840501
Humanistic & integrative, Gestalt
IAHIP

FRASER, Teresa
7 Lisfennel Close,
Dungarvan,
Co Waterford.
Tel: 058-43191
Systemic family therapy
FTAI

✓FRAWLEY, Angela
The Healing Road Clinic,
1 Flood Street,
Galway.
Tel: 091-755998
Biodynamic & integrative psychotherapy
IAHIP

✓ FRAWLEY, Michael
The Healing Road Clinic,
2nd Floor, 1 Flood Street,
Galway.
Tel: 091-755998
Biodynamic & integrative psychotherapy.
IAHIP

FRENCH, Gerry
Irish Chaplaincy in Britain
near St Mellitus, Tollington Park,
London N43AG, England.
and
IFTC Centre,
14 Elmwood Avenue,
Rathgar, Dublin 6.
Tel: 0044-171-2631477
Psychoanalytic psychotherapist
IFPP

FULTON, Linda
Family Therapy & Counselling Centre,
46 Elmwood Avenue Lwr.,
Ranelagh, Dublin 6.
Tel: 01-4971188/4971722
*Integrative, humanistic psychotherapy,
family therapy work with individuals,
couples & families.*
IAHIP & FTAI

GAFFNEY, Delia
Lucena Clinic, Blessington Road,
Tallaght, Dublin 24.
Tel: 01-4526333
Family therapy/constructivist therapy.
FTAI

GALLIGAN, Patricia
St Vincent's Hospital,
Richmond Road,
Fairview, Dublin 3.
Tel: 01-8375101
Individual & family therapy
ICPA

GARLAND, Clive
Clanwilliam Institute,
18 Clanwilliam Terrace, Dublin 2.
Tel: 01-6761363
Group analysis
IGAS

GILL, Anne
151 Ard na Mara,
Malahide, Co Dublin.
Tel: 01-8450698
*Pre & peri natal, shock & trauma,
menopause.*
IAHIP

GILL, Margaret
Dept. of Child & Family Psychiatry,
Mater Hospital,
N.C.R., Dublin 7.
Tel: 01-8034793
Systemic family therapy.
FTAI

GILLILAND, Kay P.
7 Beaver Row,
Donnybrook, Dublin 4.
Tel: 01-2691716
Bereavement/transition counselling; family therapy & supervision of same; deep tissue work.
FTAI

GILMARTIN, Helen
17 Farrenboley Park,
Dundrum,
Dublin 14.
Tel: 01-2951210
Humanistic & integrative
IAHIP

GLEESON, Betty
13 Lower Baggot Street,
Dublin 2.
Tel: 01-6775423
Psychoanalytic & systemic.
IFPP & FTAI

GORDON, Evelyn
St Joseph's Adolescent & Family
Services,
193 Richmond Road,
Fairview, Dublin 3
Tel: 01-8370802/8370448
Adolescent & family/couples therapy.
FTAI

GRIEVE, Karen
Lyradoon Family Centre,
65 Lower Salthill,
Galway.
Tel: 091-521059
Psychoanalytic psychotherapy
IFPP

GRIMLEY, Carmel
2 Manor Rise,
Grange Road,
Dublin 16.
Tel: 01-4944441
Humanistic/psychosynthesis/transpersonal
IAHIP

GRINDLEY, Geraldine M.
48 The Pines,
Howth Road, Dublin 5.
Tel: 01-8328016
Humanistic & integrative, group psychotherapy & training
IAHIP

GROSSMAN FREYNE, Gail
46 Elmwood Avenue Lr,
Ranelagh,
Dublin 6.
Tel: 01-4971188/4971722
Individual & couples therapy - mediation.
FTAI

GROVER, Mary
Ardralla,
Church Cross,
Skibbereen,
Co Cork.
Tel: 028-38373
Psychoanalytic with Jungian ethos.
IFPP

GUNNE, Dorothy
National Training & Development
Institute,
Roslyn Park, Beach Road,
Sandymount, Dublin 4.
Tel: 01-2057343
Constructivist, humanistic/systemic family therapy.
FTAI & ICPA

HAGAN, Patricia
3 Holly Park,
Dundalk,
Co Louth.
Tel: 042-26940
Humanistic & integrative psychotherapy.
IAHIP

HAMILL, Carmel
1 Ballinure Crescent,
Mahon, Cork.
Tel: 021-358372
Gestalt psychotherapist.
IAHIP

HARGIN, Mary Rose
Naas, Celbridge
& Blackrock, Co Dublin
Tel: 045-869261
Children & adolescents.
IFCAP

HARRINGTON, Eileen
11 Silverwood,
Ballinlough, Cork.
Tel: 021-295424
Gestalt
IAHIP

HAUGHTON, Helen
Rockspring,
Sandyford,
Co Dublin.
Tel: 01-2956243
Ageing/prisons
FTAI

HAYES, Fran
Laragh Counselling Service,
140 St. Lawrence's Road,
Clontarf, Dublin 3.
Tel: 01-8335044
Adult survivors of sexual abuse (individual & group therapy).
FTAI

HEALY, Daniel Christopher
Deerpark CBS,
St Patrick's Road, Cork.
Tel: 021-962025
Holistic growth/development
IAHIP

HEALY, Donal,
6 Sidney Place,
Wellington Road, Cork.
Tel: 021-507247
Integrative
IAHIP

HEGARTY, Donal
EHB, Strand House,
3 Philipsburgh Avenue,
Fairview, Dublin 3.
Tel: 01-8369899
Family therapist - family therapist supervisor
FTAI

HEGARTY, Owen
Mercers Health Centre,
Lower Stephen Street, Dublin 2.
Tel: 01-4022300
Humanistic/integrative with individuals.
IAHIP

HERLIHY, Marie
7 Brookville Estate,
Glanmire, Co Cork.
Tel: 021-821774
Awareness therapy.
IAHIP

HESKIN, Christina
'Bethesda',
Mall House,
Tuam, Co. Galway.
Tel: 093-28300
Person-centred & eclectic
IAHIP

HILL, Rosemary
Gorey Health Centre,
Hospital Grounds,
Gorey, Co Wexford.
Tel: 055-21374
Child & adolescent
IAHIP

HIRST, Iain J.
Markievicz House,
Barracks Street, Sligo.
Tel: 071-55120
Systemic: individual, couples & family therapy.
FTAI

HOLLAND, Mary
St Vincent's Hospital,
Fairview,
Dublin 3.
Tel: 01-8375101
Family therapist.
FTAI

HONNAY, Emiel
Dublin Counselling & Therapy Centre,
41 Upper Gardiner Street,
Dublin 1.
Tel: 01-8788236
Eclectic, humanistic & integrative approach with specific interest in pre- & perinatal & transpersonal psychotherapy.
IAHIP

HORNER, Carol
21 Wandsworth Road,
Belfast BT4 3LS
Northern Ireland.
Tel: 01232-653651
Humanistic & integrative
IAHIP

HOULIHAN, Tom
St Vincent's Hospital,
Fairview,
Dublin 3.
Tel: 01-8375101
Family therapy/counselling
FTAI

HOWARD, Leslie
13 Mary Street, Drogheda, Co. Louth.
and
Duile Counselling Centre,
Celbridge, Co.Kildare.
and
St Benedict's Resource Centre,
Kilbarrack, D 5.
Tel: 01-8670167
Family therapy.
FTAI

HOWLETT, Brian

Dublin Counselling & Therapy
Centre,
41 Upr. Gardiner Street,
Dublin 1.
Tel: 01-8788236
*Gestalt- for individuals & couples;
psychotherapy supervision.*
IAHIP

HUGHES, Maria

Psychological Services,
Monaghan.
Tel: 087-647588
Family therapy.
FTAI

HUMPHREYS, Vincent

189 Upper Kilmacud Road,
Stillorgan,
Co Dublin.
Tel: 01-2886145
*Gestalt therapy, individuals, couples,
groups.*
IAHIP & FTAI

HUNTER, Alison I.

28 Beech Court,
Killiney, Co Dublin.
Tel: 01-2850976
Pre & perinatal psychotherapy.
IAHIP

JACKSON, Caitriona

Aistear, Centre for Humanistic &
Integrative Psychotherapy &
Counselling,
56 Percy Lane, Ballsbridge,
Dublin 4.
Tel: 01-6675959
*Humanistic & integrative with person
centred bodywork, Gestalt, holotropic,
breathwork, transpersonal - also supervi-
sion & training.*
IAHIP

JEBB, Winston

Teen Counselling,
37 Greenfort Gardens,
Quarryvale,Clondalkin,
Dublin 22.
Tel: 01-6231398 (Mon-Thurs)
Family therapy with adolescent focus.
FTAI

JENNINGS, Norman

St John of God Hospital,
Stillorgan,
Co Dublin.
Tel: 01-2881781 Ext. 311,
Psychoanalytic psychotherapy
IFPP

JONES, Coleen

Suite 2, South Terrace Medical Centre,
Infirmary Road,
Cork.
Tel: 021-813285 / 086-8200256
*Integrative, all ages, with particular focus
on teens & health related issues.*
IAHIP

JONES, Helen

82 Upper Georges Street,
Dun Laoghaire, Co Dublin.
Tel: 01-2802523
*Humanistic & integrative psychothera-
pist & trainer - individual & group
work.*
IAHIP

JOYCE, Nora

The Healing House,
24 O'Connell Avenue,
Berkeley Road,
Dublin 7.
Tel: 01-4964940
*Humanistic & integrative approach with
use of creative methods & also the possi-
bility of working through French.*
IAHIP

JUDGE, Jimmy
Rutland Centre,
Knocklyon Road,
Templeogue,
Dublin 16.
Tel: 01-4946358
Addiction, family dynamics, inner child work, humanistic & integrative.
IAHIP

JUTHAN, Kay
EHB, Glenmalure Day Hospital,
Milltown Road,
Dublin 6.
Tel: 01-2830388
Family/marital therapist, biofeedback therapist RPN.
FTAI

KEANE, Verena
Clanwilliam Institute,
18 Clanwilliam Terrace,
Dublin 2.
Tel: 01-6761363
Systemic therapy.
FTAI

KEARNEY, Philip
Clanwilliam Institute,
18 Clanwilliam Terrace,
Dublin 2.
Tel: 01-6761363
Systemic family therapy
FTAI

KEARNEY, Ruth
5 Beechlawn,
South Hill Avenue,
Blackrock,
Co Dublin.
Tel: 01-2833724
Jungian psychoanalytic psychotherapy
IFPP

KEENAN, Marie
Granada Institute,
Crinken House,
Crinken Lane,
Shankill, Co Dublin.
Tel: 01-2721030
Systemic & narrative therapy.
FTAI

KEHOE, Helen
11 Stockton Park,
Castleknock,
Dublin 15.
Tel: 01-8216836
Humanistic, integrative, eclectic.
IAHIP

KEIGHER, Marian
Castle Street,
Roscommon.
Tel: 0903-26124
Family therapist.
FTAI

KELLEHER, Kathleen
Mater Dei Counselling Centre,
Clonliffe Road,
Dublin 3.
Tel: 01-8371892
Family therapy
FTAI

KELLIHER, Anne
8 Springfort, Montenotte, Cork
and
4 Cedar Court, Ashleigh Downs,
Tralee
Co Kerry.
Tel: 021-551031(Cork)
066-20142 (Kerry)
Relationships, survivors of childhood traumas, bereavement, depression.
IAHIP

KENNEDY, Jo
Hesed House,
74 Tyrconnell Road,
Inchicore,
Dublin 8.
Tel: 01-4549474
Family systemic therapy.
FTAI

KIERNAN, Donal
24 Parnell Road,
Bray,
Co Wicklow.
Tel: 01-2868614
Abuse/addiction, issues of love & loss in childhood & death.
IAHIP

KILCOYNE, Phyllis
Family Institute,
Ballaghaderreen,
Co Roscommon.
Tel: 0907-61000
Individual, marital & family therapy.
FTAI

KILGALLEN, Aideen
Rape Crisis Centre,
70 Lower Leeson Street,
Dublin 2.
Tel: 01-6614911
IAHIP

KILLORAN-GANNON, Sheila
43 Belgrave Square West,
Rathmines,
Dublin 6.
Tel: 01-4960545
Humanistic & integrative psychotherapy: adults, adolescents.
IAHIP

KING, Margaret
Newtownsmith,
Galway.
Tel: 091-563698
Individual & family therapy.
IAHIP

KIRK, Geraldine
Clonard House,
The Square,
Navan,
Co Meath.
Tel: 046-71648
Family therapy.
FTAI

KOHNSTAMM, Barbara
5 Tivoli Terrace East,
Dun Laoghaire,
Co Dublin.
Tel: 01- 2803789
Individual, couples & families; integrative psychotherapist.
FTAI & IAHIP

KRZECZUNOWICZ, Sarah E. (Kay)
2, Longwood Avenue,
off Sth. Circular Road,
Dublin 8.
Tel: 01-4530344
Gestalt therapist - specialist in voice work.
IAHIP

LALOR, Mary
Duile Counselling Psychotherapy Centre,
Maynooth Road,
Celbridge, Co Kildare.
Tel: 01-6273909
Individual, couple & family therapy; assistance in dealing with trauma, phobias, abuse, stress, relationships, addictions, loneliness, depression.
FTAI

LEE, Mary
Vita House,
Abbey Street,
Roscommon.
Tel: 0903-25898
Family therapy
FTAI

LESLIE, Frank
7 Broadway Park,
Blanchardstown,
Dublin 15.
Tel: 01-8214022
Family therapist.
FTAI

LEWIS, Maeve
New Day Counselling Centre,
11 Meath Street,
Dublin 8.
Tel: 01-4547050
Post-traumatic stress, sexual abuse from a humanistic/integrative perspective.
IAHIP

LIDDY, Rosemary
Milltown Medical Clinic,
98 Lower Churchtown Road,
Dublin 14.
Tel: 01-2960918
Work with adults, adolescents, groups, supervision, specialising in PTSD, childhood abuse, humanistic approach.
IAHIP

LINDEN, Mairead
1 Ballinure Crescent,
Mahon,
Cork.
Tel: 021-358372
Adult Gestalt psychotherapist.
IAHIP

LINDSAY, John
Connect Associates,
Lonsdale House,
Avoca Avenue,
Blackrock,
Co Dublin.
Tel: 01-2884155
Working with individuals, couples & groups, supervisory- special interest in bioenergetics with individuals & groups.
IAHIP

LINDSAY, Susan
Connect Associates,
Lonsdale House,
Avoca Avenue,
Blackrock, Co Dublin.
Tel: 01-2884155
Humanistic & integrative with individuals & groups.
IAHIP

LINNANE, Paul
Smithfield Chambers,
Smithfield, Dublin 7
Tel: 01-8733722
Family therapy.
FTAI

LOGAN, Paddy
Aistear,
56 Percy Lane,
Ballsbridge, Dublin 4.
Tel: 01-6675959
Client centred, Gestalt, biodynamic, analytic - individual & group work - also supervision.
IAHIP

LONERGAN, Mary-Anna
108 Spring Road,
Letchworth,
Herts SG6 3SL.
Gestalt
IAHIP

LOUGHLIN, Paula
21 Cowper Road,
Rathmines, Dublin 6.
Tel: 01-4966766
Individual psychotherapy grounded in psychosynthesis.
IAHIP

LUCEY, Joe
Salesian Youth Enterprises,
72 Sean Mc Dermott Street,
Dublin 1.
Tel: 01-8558792
Constructivist; systemic; young people; addiction.
ICPA

LYNCH, Catherine
16 Ard na Meala,
Ballymun, Dublin 11.
Tel: 01-8426534
Humanistic integrative.
IAHIP

MAC GUINNESS, Irene
EHB, Basin Street,
Naas, Co Kildare.
Tel: 045-876001 / 874006
Systemic family therapy, humanistic & integrative psychotherapy.
FTAI

MAC NAMARA, Vincent
Eckhart House,
19 Clyde Road, Dublin 4.
Tel: 01-6684687
Psychosynthesis-psychodynamic
IAHIP

MAC NEILL, Sile
Baltyboys,
Blessington, Co Wicklow.
Tel: 045-867218
Gestalt
IAHIP

MADDEN, Joan
Knockanrawley Resource Centre,
Tipperary Town,
Co Tipperary.
Tel: 062-52688
Individual, couples & family therapy.
FTAI

MAGEE, David Louis
10 Park Villas,
Castleknock,
Dublin 15.
Tel: 01-8211650
Psychiatrist & psychotherapist - individuals & couples.
ICPA

MAGENIS, Maire
Regional Child & Family Health Service,
NWHB General Hospital,
Letterkenny,
Co Donegal.
Tel: 074-25888 Ext: 2588
Family therapy.
FTAI

MAGUIRE, Una
Institute of Creative Counselling & Psychotherapy,
82 Upper George's Street,
Dun Laoghaire,
Co Dublin.
Tel: 01-2802523
Humanistic & integrative psychotherapy, supervision & training.
IAHIP

MAHER, Ann
35 Woodquay,
Galway City.
Tel: 091-522124 / 087-2436896
Biodynamic & integrative psychotherapy.
IAHIP

MAHER, Bonnie
136 Morehampton Road,
Donnybrook, Dublin 4.
Tel: 01-4964799
Psychoanalytic psychotherapy.
IFPP

MAHER, Pascal
Greenlea Clinic,
118 Greenlea Road, Dublin 6W.
Tel: 01-4908979/4502669
Individual, couple & family therapy.
FTAI

MANDOS, Koos
Mater Child & Family Centre,
Ballymun Shopping Centre,
Dublin 11.
Tel: 01-8420319
Family therapy.
FTAI

MANNION WALSHE, Deirdre
'Avalon', 8 Alma Park,
Monkstown Village, Co Dublin.
Tel: 01-2845208
Humanistic & integrative psychotherapy.
IAHIP

MARTIN, Maeve
Community Care Centre,
South Eastern Health Board,
Clonmel, Co Tipperary.
Tel: 052-22011 (W) 052-24235 (H)
Child & adolescent psychotherapy.
IFCAP

MARTIN, Ray
Belgrave Avenue,
Wellington Road, Cork.
Tel: 021-505393
Holistic awareness therapy with individuals & groups.
IAHIP

MASTERSON, Ingrid
'Alberta',
Ardtona Avenue,
Lr. Churchtown Road,
Dublin 14.
Tel: 01-2988288
Psychoanalytic psychotherapy (UKCP registered)
IFPP

MATHEWS, Peter
St Davnet's Hospital,
Monaghan,
Co Monaghan.
Tel: 047-81822
Behavioural psychotherapy
CBT

MC ADAM, Frank
St Davnet's Hospital,
Monaghan,
Co Monaghan.
Tel: 047-81822
Behavioural & cognitive therapy with adults.
CBT

MC ALEER, Jennifer
Rosemount Centre,
60 Clare Street,
Limerick.
Tel: 061-415697
Family therapy.
FTAI

MC CARRICK, Tom
North Western Health Board,
Ballytivnan,
Sligo.
Tel: 071-42111
Psychoanalytic psychotherapy & group analysis
IFPP

MC CARTHY, Anne
129 Cosgrave Park,
Moyross, Limerick.
Tel: 061-452511
Psychosynthesis
IAHIP

MC CARTHY, Dan
3 Knocknamona Park,
Letterkenny, Co Donegal.
Tel: 074-22774
Gestalt psychotherapy
IAHIP

MC CARTHY, Imelda
Vico Consultation Centre,
2 Dungar Terrace,
Dun Laoghaire, Co Dublin.
Tel: 01-2843336
Systemic - social constructionist.
FTAI

MC CARTHY, Ros
Clonsast,
Kilcock, Co Kildare.
Tel: 01-6287005
Family & psychoanalytic psychotherapy.
FTAI

MC CASHIN, Dolores
39 Belgard Downs,
Rochestown Road, Cork.
Tel: 021-892169
Humanistic/integrative
IAHIP

MC COURT, Ann
Trinity Counselling Service,
House 6, Trinity College,
Dublin 2.
Tel: 01-6081407
Psychoanalytic & body oriented psychother-
apy with particular interest in addic-
tions, eating disorders & sexual abuse.
IAHIP

MC COURT, Marie
206 Moyville,
Rathfarnham, Dublin 16.
Tel: 01-4945818
General counselling-sexual identity.
IAHIP

MC CULLY, Maria
Clondalkin Addiction Support
Programme,
37 Greenfort Gardens,
Quarryvale, Clondalkin,
Dublin 22.
Tel: 01-6230100/6237752/6237753
Systemic family/community approach;
addiction counselling - all from a hu-
manistic & integrative approach.
IAHIP

MC FADDEN, Hugh
'Sancta Maria',
Gortlee, Letterkenny,
Co Donegal.
Tel: 074-21919
Cognitive & behavioural, dealing with a
wide range of emotional & behavioural
problems which include phobias, stress,
PTSD, psychosexual problems, sexual
abuse, depression, etc.
CBT

MC GEE, Breda
35 Brompton Court, Dublin 15.
Tel: 01-8225559
Family therapist, systemic family therapy
working with families, couples & indi-
viduals.
FTAI

MC GLYNN, James
North West Community Services,
Dungloe District Hospital,
Dungloe, Co Donegal.
Tel: 075-21044
Behavioural psychotherapist
CBT

MC GLYNN, Peter
Mental Health Centre,
Maginn Avenue,
Buncrana,
Co Donegal.
Tel: 077-61500
Behavioural psychotherapies for acute adult mental health problems.
CBT

MC GOLDRICK, Mary
St Patrick's Hospital,
James' Street,
Dublin 8.
Tel: 01-6775423 Ext. 402.
Behavioural psychotherapy.
CBT

MC GRATH, Terri
9 Diamond Hill,
Monkstown, Co Cork.
and
Friary Court, Friary Street, Kilkenny.
Tel: 021-841754 and 056-65613
Individual, couple & family relationship consultant.
FTAI

MC GROARY-MEEHAN, Maureen
East End House,
Clar Road,
Donegal Community Services,
Donegal Town.
Tel: 073-21933
CBT

MC HALE, Edmund
Clanwilliam Institute,
18 Clanwilliam Terrace,
Dublin 2.
Tel: 01-6761363/6762881
Couple & family therapy.
FTAI

MC HUGH, Charles
Tirconaill House,
St Conal's Hospital,
Letterkenny, Co Donegal.
Tel: 074-21022
Anxiety states, stress, phobias, sexual dysfunction, PTSD, chronic fatigue syndrome, eating disorders, obsessive compulsive disorders.
CBT

MC KEE, Maud
Tel: 01-8730700 Ext.343/6234169
ICPA

MC LEAVEY, Bernadette
12 Granville Crescent,
Cabinteely, Co Dublin.
Tel: 01-2847037
Art therapy.
IAHIP

MC LOONE, Anne
Family Enrichment Centre,
Stranorlar, Co Donegal.
Tel: 074-31245
Systemic family therapy, family & marital therapist, including personal therapy.
FTAI

MC LOUGHLIN, Sarah
Clanwilliam Institute,
18 Clanwilliam Terrace,
off Grand Canal Quay,
Dublin 2.
Tel: 01-6761363
Family (systems) therapist.
FTAI

MC MANUS, Libby
Rosemary Square,
Roscrea, Co. Tipperary.
Tel: 0505-21222
Family therapy working with individuals, couples & families.
FTAI

MC MORROW, Mary
Mental Health Centre,
Markievicz House,
Sligo.
Tel: 071-55100
Family & couples therapy.
FTAI

MC QUAID, Margaret
St Mary's,
Laytown,
Co Meath.
Tel: 041-27271
Humanistic & integrative - bodywork & Gestalt; holotropic breathwork.
IAHIP

MEAGHER, Kathleen A.
Fortune House,
Cherry Orchard Hospital,
Ballyfermot,
Dublin 10.
Tel: 087-2624140 / 01-6232200
Humanistic/ integrative, person-centred.
IAHIP

MEEK, Pauline
52 Dargle Road,
Hollypark,
Blackrock,
Co Dublin.
Tel: 01-2896435
Systemic therapist- couples, step-families & step-parenting issues.
FTAI

MELVIN PERREM, Breda
3 Sydenham Terrace,
Monkstown,
Co Cork.
Tel: 021-842087
Adult psychotherapy
IAHIP

MOHALLY, Derry
6 Sydney Place,
Wellington Road,
Cork.
Tel: 021-507247
Integrative psychotherapy - individuals, couples & groups.
IAHIP

MOLEY, Patrick
Ladywell Centre,
Louth County Hospital,
Dundalk,
Co Louth.
Tel: 042-26156
Systemic family therapist.
FTAI

MONAGHAN, Ann
Family Therapy Svcs, Markievicz
House, Sligo
and
Regional Child & Family Service, Out
Patient Dept, Sligo General Hospital.
Tel: 071-71111 Ext. 4350
Family & couples therapy
FTAI

MONAGHAN, Theresa
Aisling Centre,
37 Darling Street, Enniskillen,
Co Fermanagh.
Tel: 01365-325811
CQSW, registered marital/family therapist.
FTAI

MOONEY, Alan A.
Centre for Creative Change,
14 Upper Clanbrassil Street,
Dublin 8.
Tel: 01-4538356 (W) 8491887 (H)
Humanistic & integrative.
IAHIP

MOONEY MC GLOIN, Catherine
Cregg House,
Rosses Point Road,
Sligo.
Tel: 071-77229
Behaviour therapy for people with learning disabilities.
CBT

MOORE, Lucy M.
Cluain Mhuire Family Centre,
Newtownpark Avenue,
Blackrock,
Co Dublin.
Tel: 01-2833766
Systemic therapy.
FTAI

MORRISON, Anne
Markievicz House,
Barrack Street,
Sligo.
Tel: 071-55120
Family & marital therapy.
FTAI

MOUNTAIN, Jane
The Acupuncture & Psychotherapy Clinic,
26 Upper John Street,
Kilkenny.
Tel: 056-58639
Humanistic; transpersonal; biodynamic.
IAHIP

MOYLAN, Bernadette
Newpark House,
Kiltoom,
Athlone,
Co Roscommon.
Tel: 0902-89421/89333
Biodynamic & integrative.
IAHIP

MULHERE, Jacinta
St Vincent's Centre,
Navan Road,
Dublin 7.
Tel: 01-8383234
Behaviour therapy for people with learning disabilities with particular interest in challenging behaviour.
CBT

MULHOLLAND, Marie Therese
St Patrick's Hospital,
James Street,
Dublin 8.
Tel: 01-6775423
Systemic family therapy.
FTAI

MULLER, Elisabeth
Turning Point,
23 Crofton Road,
Dun Laoghaire,
Co Dublin.
Tel: 01-2800626/2807888
Humanistic & integrative.
IAHIP

MURNANE, Eilis
2 Liscarne Gardens,
Rowlagh,
Clondalkin,
Dublin 22.
Tel: 01-6263077
Family therapy
FTAI

MURPHY, Ann C.
120 Leinster Road,
Dublin 6.
Tel: 01-4973080
Psychoanalytic psychotherapy
IFPP

MURPHY, Brendan
Arduna Counselling & Psychotherapy Centre,
55 Clontarf Road,
Dublin 3.
Tel: 01-8332733
Psychoanalytic psychotherapy.
IFPP

MURPHY, David
43 Main Street, Swords, Co Dublin.
and
26 Longford Tce., Monkstown, Co Dublin.
Tel: 01-8901494
Humanistic, integrative & transpersonal plus biodynamic, body analysis & massage.
IAHIP

MURPHY, Ger
Institute of Creative Counselling & Psychotherapy,
82 Upper George's Street,
Dun Laoghaire,
Co Dublin.
Tel: 01-2802523
Integrative psychotherapist - bodywork-analytic
IAHIP

MURPHY, Mary
25 Glasnevin Hill,
Glasnevin, Dublin 9.
Tel: 01-8368966
Individual, couple & family therapy.
FTAI

MURPHY ROCHE, Freda
46 Elmwood Avenue Lower,
Ranelagh, Dublin 6.
Tel: 01-4971188 / 4971722
Continuing body work (Trager massage, process acupressure) with psychotherapy.
FTAI

MURRAY, Claire
6 Sidney Place,
Wellington Road, Cork.
Tel: 021-507247
Integrative
IAHIP

MURRAY, Denis
Fortune House,
Cherryorchard Hospital,
Cherryorchard, Dublin 10.
Tel: 01-6237356
Systemic therapy with individuals, couples & families - specialising in addiction & work with young people.
FTAI

MURRAY, Janet
Tivoli Institute,
24 Clarinda Park East,
Dun Laoghaire, Co. Dublin.
Tel: 01-2809178
Psychoanalytic
IFCAP

MURRAY, Marie
St Vincent's Psychiatric Hospital &
St Joseph's Adolescent Services,
Richmond Road,
Fairview, Dublin 3.
Tel: 01-8370802 / 2885517
Family, adolescent
FTAI

MYERS, Gerry
Pastoral Centre, Denmark St, Limerick
and
1 St Flannan's St, Nenagh,
Co Tipperary.
Tel: 067-33280 / 086-8170380
Integrative psychotherapist; general therapy for individuals, couples, groups, teenagers & adults; special areas: depression, psychosexual issues.
IAHIP

NANNERY, Teresa

General Hospital, Sligo
and
The Lodge, Villa Nova, West End,
Bundoran, Co Donegal.
Tel: 072-41818
Humanistic/integrative psychotherapy,
post mastectomy therapy.
IAHIP

NEARY, Nora

Lucena Clinic,
Century Court,
Dun Laoghaire,
Co Dublin.
Tel: 01-2801204 (H) 2809809 (W)
Psychoanalytic psychotherapy in child &
adolescent psychotherapy.
IFCAP

NÍ CHONAOLA, Mairead

8 Beech Park,
Renmore, Galway.
Tel: 091-753015
Humanistic & integrative
IAHIP

NÍ GHALLCHOBHAIR, Maighread

1 Mount Merrion Avenue,
Blackrock,
Co Dublin.
Tel: 01-2887066
Child & adolescent psychoanalytic psy-
chotherapy.
IFCAP

NÍ NUALLÁIN, Mairin

Augustine Court,
Augustine Street,
Galway.
Tel: 091-567035
Psychiatrist: Jungian psychotherapist &
group analyst.
IFPP & IGAS

NÍ UALLACHÁIN, Meabh

'St Louis',
Blakestown Road,
Mulhuddart,
Dublin 15.
Tel: 01-8217432
Humanistic & integrative with special
interests in groupwork, Gestalt & areas
of depression. Work with married, single
& religious - men & women.
IAHIP

NOLAN, Declan

Dr Steevens Hospital,
Dublin 8.
Tel: 01-6790700
Family therapy.
FTAI

NOLAN, Inger

26 Longford Terrace,
Monkstown,
Co Dublin.
Tel: 01-2809313
Integrative psychotherapy, use of art,
family therapy.
IAHIP & FTAI

NOLAN, Maeve

LSB College,
Balfe Street,
Dublin 2.
Tel: 01-4960472
Psychoanalysis
IFPP

NOLAN, Patrick

26 Longford Terrace,
Monkstown,
Co Dublin.
Tel: 01-2809313
Psychoanalytic & integrative
IFPP & IAHIP

O'BRIEN, David.
Group Analytic Practice,
29 Lower Abbey Street, Dublin 1.
Tel: 01-8786486
Group analysis.
IGAS

O'BRIEN, Gay
1 Auburn Drive,
Castleknock, Dublin 15.
Tel: 01-8217548
Constructivist psychotherapist
ICPA & FTAI

O'BRIEN, Jim
St Brigid's Hospital,
Ardee, Co Louth.
Tel: 041-53264 (W) 042-63743 (H)
Systemic family therapist.
FTAI

O'BRIEN, Tom
Jonathan Swift Clinic, Dept of
Psychiatry,
St James' Hospital,
Dublin 8.
Tel: 01-4537941 Ext. 2621
Family therapist working with individuals, couples, families & mental illness.
FTAI

O'BRIEN, Valerie
Clanwilliam Institute,
18 Clanwilliam Terrace, Dublin 2.
Tel: 01-6761363
Systemic, family, couples & children.
FTAI

O'CONNOR, Colm J.
Cork & Ross Family Centre,
34 Paul Street, Cork.
Tel: 021-275678
Clinical psychology; integrative family therapy.
FTAI

O'CONNOR, Elizabeth
52 Castlepark Road,
Sandycove,
Co Dublin.
Tel: 01-2857459
Group analysis.
IGAS

O'CONNOR, Karen E.
Walmer House,
Station Road,
Raheny,
Dublin 5.
Tel: 01-8327859
Humanistic & integrative
IAHIP

O'CONNOR, Marika
'Sanctuary',
Lanesville,
Monkstown,
Co Dublin.
Tel: 01-2809964
Integrative, with a special interest in object-relations therapy.
IAHIP

O'DALAIGH, Liam
12 Elmbrook Avenue,
Lucan,
Co Dublin.
Tel: 01-6241955
Marital & family therapy.
FTAI

O'DEA, Catherine
Eglinton House,
Eglinton Terrace,
Dundrum,
Dublin 14.
Tel: 01-2986204
Humanistic & integrative psychotherapy with individuals, & supervision.
IAHIP

O'DEA, Eileen
'Shalom' Therapy Suite,
5 Chapel Street,
Castlebar,
Co Mayo.
Tel: 094-25142
Systemic/family therapy with families,
couples & individuals.
FTAI

O'DOHERTY, Colm
ICCP,
82 Upper George's Street,
Dun Laoghaire,
Co Dublin.
Tel: 01-2802523
Integrative psychotherapy - individual &
couple; supervision & training.
IAHIP

O'DONNELL, Godfrey
Eastern Health Board,
140 St Laurence's Road,
Clontarf,
Dublin 3.
Tel: 01-8338252
Systemic constructivist.
ICPA

O'DONNELL, Ruth
EHB, Strand House,
3 Philipsburgh Avenue,
Fairview,
Dublin 3.
Tel: 01-8369899 (answering machine)
Systemic/constructivist - supervisor.
FTAI

O'DONOGHUE, Eilis
3 Larkfield Gardens,
Harold's Cross,
Dublin 6W
Tel: 01-4922653
Humanistic & integrative.
IAHIP

O'DONOGHUE, Jim
Kedron, St Mary's Road, Edenderry,
Co Offaly
and
Dublin Counselling & Therapy Centre,
41 Upper Gardiner Street, Dublin 1.
Tel: 0405-33311 and 01-8788236
Psycho-dynamic & transpersonal psy-
chotherapy with a client-centred ap-
proach.
IAHIP

O'DONOGHUE, Paul
Dublin Counselling & Therapy
Centre,
41 Upper Gardiner Street,
Dublin 1.
Tel: 01-8788236
Person-centred; eclectic; systemic.
IAHIP

O'DONOVAN, Joan
Eckhart House,
19 Clyde Road, Dublin 4.
Tel: 01-6684687
Psychosynthesis
IAHIP

O'DONOVAN, Mairin
'Tara',
Knockenpaddin,
Dunmore East,
Co Waterford.
Tel: 051-383842
Marital & family therapy.
FTAI

O'DONOVAN, Margot
5 Sycamore Walk,
The Park, Cabinteely,
Co Dublin.
Tel: 01-2849605
Humanistic integrative psychotherapy.
IAHIP

O'DOWD, Maura
12 O'Connor's Terrace,
Boherbee,
Tralee, Co Kerry
Tel: 088-2618647
Bio-dynamic & integrative - supervision.
IAHIP

O'DUFFY, Ann
New Day Counselling Centre,
11 Meath Street, Dublin 8.
Tel: 01-4547050
Humanistic integrative psychotherapy.
IAHIP

O'DWYER, Mary
Mercy House,
Clonard Road, Wexford.
Tel: 053-23024
Humanistic & integrative.
IAHIP

O'FLAHERTY, Anne
St Louise's Unit,
Our Lady's Hospital,
Crumlin, Dublin 12.
Tel: 01-4558220
Child & adolescent psychotherapy
IFCAP

O'GRADY, Ethna
Family Institute,
Ballaghaderreen, Co Roscommon.
Tel: 0907-61000
Individual, marital & family therapy.
FTAI

O'HALLORAN, Mary
10 Woodcliff Heights,
Howth, Co Dublin.
Tel: 01-8325004
*Individual counselling, also couples work,
Gestalt therapist, special interest in
dreamwork.*
IAHIP

O'HALLORAN, Mike
Dubh Linn Institute,
16 Prospect Road,
Glasnevin,
Dublin 9.
Tel: 01-8302358
Gestalt for individuals & couples.
IAHIP

O'HANLON, Judy
Dundrum Gestalt Centre,
Park House, Eglington Terrace,
Upper Kilmacud Road, Dublin 14.
Tel: 01-2962015
*Humanist & Gestalt therapist working
with individuals, couples & groups.
Special interest in adolescence; supervi-
sion & professional support; training.*
IAHIP

O'HARA, Carmel
Rock Road Psychotherapy Practice,
110 Rock Road,
Booterstown, Co Dublin.
Tel: 01-6601301 (Wk. No./Hme No.
& Answering Machine)
*Individuals, couples, families, especially
those in recovery from addictions - sys-
temic therapy. (Masters Med. Sc/psy-
chotherapy).*
FTAI

O'LEARY, Eleanor Anne
Dept. of Applied Psychology,
University College Cork.
Tel: 021-902612
Person centred Gestalt therapy.
IAHIP

O'MAHONY, Catherine
Nationwide House,
Mullingar, Co Westmeath.
Tel: 044-61104
Psychoanalyst
IFPP

O'MAHONY, Eileen
C/O EHB, Patrick Street,
Dun Laoghaire,
Co Dublin.
Tel: 01-2808403
Family therapy
FTAI

O'MAHONY, Hank
Cnoc an Glas,
An Spideal,
Co na Gaillimh.
Tel: 091-553548
Gestalt psychotherapist, supervisor &
trainer.
IAHIP

O'MAHONY, Judy
38 Ulverton Road,
Dalkey,
Co Dublin.
Tel: 01-2803405
Group analytic psychotherapy, working
with therapy groups & organisation/team
groups.
IGAS

O'MALLEY-DUNLOP, Ellen
33 Springfield Road,
Terenure, Dublin 6W
and
Mews 1, 73 Pembroke Lane
Dublin 4.
Tel: 01-4904879
Individual psychotherapist with a
Jungian orientation - group analyst.
IFPP IGAS FTAI

O'NEILL, Ann
Fahy Law Offices,
John Street,
Limerick.
Tel: 061-454736
Humanistic & integrative.
IAHIP

O'NEILL, Breege
Bethesda,
Mall House,
Tuam,
Co Galway.
Tel: 093-28300
Systemic family therapist working with
individuals, couples, families.
FTAI

O'NEILL, Deborah
Caherkelly,
Ardrahan,
Co Galway.
Tel: 091-635112
Transpersonal psychotherapy using a con-
templative approach.
IAHIP

O'NEILL, Elizabeth
Mid Western Health Board,
Pearse Street,
Nenagh,
Co Tipperary.
Tel: 067-31212
Marital/family systems; personal therapy
including addictions counselling.
FTAI

O'NEILL, Julia
Kilbeacanty,
Gort,
Co Galway.
Tel: 091-631164
Biodynamic psychotherapist.
IAHIP

O'NEILL, Mary
New Day Counselling Centre,
11 Meath Street,
Dublin 8.
Tel: 01-4547050
Humanistic & integrative
IAHIP

O'NEILL, Nora
7 Woodbrook,
Rochestown Road,
Cork.
Tel: 021-362068
Integrative
IAHIP

O'REILLY, Anne
77a Marlborough Road,
Donnybrook,
Dublin 4.
Tel: 01-4976140 / 087-556335
Constructivist
ICPA

O'REILLY, Joseph
St Joseph's,
Ferryhouse,
Clonmel,
Co Tipperary.
Tel: 052-24633
Humanistic, integrative.
IAHIP

O'REILLY, Maureen
Eckhart House,
19 Clyde Road,
Dublin 4.
Tel: 01-6684687
Psychosynthesis; psycho-dynamic.
IAHIP

O'ROURKE, Darina
4 Pembroke Cottages,
PYE Centre, Ballinteer Road,
Dundrum,
Dublin 14.
Tel: 01-2962115
Humanistic & integrative.
IAHIP

O'SCOLLAIN, Eibhlin
St John of God Hospital,
Stillorgan,
Co Dublin.
Tel: 01-2881781 Ext. 252
Systemic - individual, couples & family therapy.
FTAI

O'SHAUGHNESSY, Marie
Hesed House,
74 Tyrconnell Road,
Inchicore,
Dublin 8.
Tel: 01-4549474
Family/systemic therapy.
FTAI

O'SULLIVAN, Creina
Mary Street Medical Centre,
Mary Street,
Dungarvan,
Co Waterford.
Tel: 058-41162
Systemic family therapy.
FTAI

O'SULLIVAN, Marych
19 Trafalgar Terrace,
Basement,
Monkstown,
Co Dublin.
Tel: 01-2800569
Psychoanalytic psychotherapy- adult & adolescent.
IFPP & IFCAP

O'TOOLE, Muriel
6 Pepper's Court,
Fintan Lawlor Avenue,
Portlaoise,
Co Laois.
Tel: 0502-62101
Psychosynthesis
IAHIP

OWENS, Conor
6 Westbury Avenue,
Lucan,
Co Dublin.
Tel: (01) 6211223
Child & adolescent psychotherapy.
IFCAP

PARKS, Ann
Dundalk Counselling Centre,
'Oakdene', 3 Seatown Place,
Dundalk,
Co Louth.
Tel: 042-38333
IAHIP

PEAKIN, Anne
1 Woodlawn,
Upper Churchtown Road,
Dundrum,
Dublin 14.
Tel: 01-2959043
Individual - all areas excluding addictions.
IAHIP

PHALAN, Sally
The Surgery,
1 Athgoe Drive,
Shankill,
Co Dublin.
Tel: 01-2829251
Child & adolescent
IFCAP

PORTER, Sheila
Lucena Clinic,
Old Blessington Road,
Tallaght,
Dublin 24.
Tel: 01-4526333
Family therapy
FTAI

PRENDERVILLE, Mary
9 Albany Road,
Ranelagh,
Dublin 6.
Tel: 01-4973425
Gestalt & integrative psychotherapy
IAHIP

PRYLE, Fiona M.
Ruhama Womens Project,
Kilmacud House,
Upper Kilmacud Road,
Stillorgan, Co Dublin.
Tel: 01- 2835855
Family therapist.
FTAI

PYLE, Mary
31 Palmerstown Road,
Dublin 6.
Tel: 01-4973670
Group analysis; psychoanalytic psychotherapy.
IGAS & IFPP

REIDY, Margaret
Psychological Services,
Monaghan.
Tel: 087-2388537
Family therapist.
FTAI

REYNOLDS, Mary
St Vincent's Centre,
Navan Road,
Dublin 7.
Tel: 01-8383234
Behaviour therapy for people with learning disabilities with particular interest in challenging behaviour.
CBT

RICHARDSON, Anne
St Patrick's Hospital,
James' Street, Dublin 8.
Tel: 01-6775423
Systemic therapy.
FTAI

RICHARDSON, Colette
5/36 Boundary Road,
London NW8 OHG,
Tel: 0171-3724886
Systemic
FTAI

RIORDAN, Gillian
Eckhart House,
19 Clyde Road, Dublin 4.
Tel: 01-6684687
Psychosynthesis
IAHIP

ROCHE, Declan
Clanwilliam Institute,
18 Clanwilliam Terrace,
Dublin 2.
Tel: 01- 6761363 / 087-635461
Addiction, pain management, post trau-matic stress disorder (PTSD)
FTAI

ROCHE, Sile
Stanhope Centre,
Lower Grangegorman, Dublin 7.
Tel: 01-6773965
Systemic social constructionist
FTAI

ROE, Liam
Talbot Centre,
29 Upper Buckingham Street,
Dublin 1.
Tel: 01-8363434 (W), 6271301 (H)
Young people, drugs/alcohol abuse, family & individual therapy.
FTAI

ROTHERY, Nuala
Woodside,
Sandyford,
Co Dublin.
Tel: 01-2956163
Process oriented psychotherapy & relation-ship counselling.
IAHIP

RUSSELL, Maura
Rutland Centre,
Knocklyon House,
Knocklyon Road,
Dublin 16.
Tel: 01-4946358
Psychodynamic, addiction counselling.
ICPA

RUTH-MURRAY, Ann M.
Shoni,
Well Road,
Little Island,
Cork.
Tel: 021-354843
Biodynamic, humanistic & integrative.
IAHIP

RYAN, Anne
Dublin Counselling & Therapy Centre,
41 Upper Gardiner Street,
Dublin 1.
Tel: 01-8788236
Humanistic & integrative
IAHIP

RYAN, Catherine
4 Pembroke Cottages,
The PYE Centre,
Ballinteer Road, Dundrum,
Dublin 14.
Tel: 01-2962115
Humanistic & integrative & energy work.
IAHIP

RYAN, David.
New Day Counselling Centre,
11 Meath Street, Dublin 8.
Tel: 01-4547050
Humanistic/integrative.
IAHIP

RYAN, Derval
Aer Lingus Employee Assistance,
Personnel Building,
Dublin Airport,
Dublin.
Tel: 01-7052868 / 7052870
Group analytic psychotherapy/analytic psychotherapy.
IFPP & IGAS

RYAN, Mairead
Clifton House,
Lr Fitzwilliam Street, Dublin 2.
Tel: 01-6614828
Behavioural psychotherapy
CBT

RYAN, Teresa
Warrenmount Centre,
Blackpitts, Dublin 8.
Tel: 01-4542622
Humanistic & integrative
IAHIP

RYAN, Toni
16 Casimir Road,
Harold's Cross, Dublin 6W.
Tel: 01-4922447
Humanistic & integrative.
IAHIP

SAHAFI, Janet E.
87 Mountain View,
Naas, Co Kildare.
Tel: 045-894187
Psychodrama & other creative experiential techniques (individual & group).
IAHIP

SCULLY, Patricia
Stanhope Centre,
Lower Grangegorman Road,
Dublin 7.
Tel: 01-6773965
Systemic therapist.
FTAI

SELL, Patrick
Centre for Biodynamic & Integrative
Psychotherapy,
Tracht Beach,
Kinvara,
Co Galway.
Tel: 091-637192
Biodynamic & integrative psychotherapist & trainer.
IAHIP

SHEEHAN, Bartley
21 Summerhill,
Dun Laoghaire,
Co Dublin.
Tel: 01-2806908
Constructivist.
ICPA

SHEEHAN, Jim
Dept. of Child & Family Psychiatry,
Mater Hospital, Dublin 7
and
6 Windsor Road, Dublin 6.
Tel: 01-8300700 & 4964406
Systemic therapy.
FTAI

SHEEHAN, Thomas
Western Health Board,
Roscommon Community Care,
Ardsallagh,
Athlone Road,
Roscommon.
Tel: 0903-27089
Family therapy.
FTAI

SHEILL, Mary
Solace,
36 Dublin Street,
Carlow.
Tel: 0503-30611
Humanistic & integrative, eclectic, individual & groupwork, person centred & transpersonal approaches, supervision.
IAHIP

SHERIDAN, Anne
'Greenlands',
Loughnagin,
Letterkenny,
Co Donegal.
Tel: 074-27707
Teenagers & their families.
FTAI

SHIELDS, Vivienne
Family Therapy & Counselling
Centre,
46 Elmwood Avenue,
Ranelagh, Dublin 6.
Tel: 01-4971188
Family therapist.
FTAI

SHORTEN, Karen Ilean
28 Parkwood Grove,
Aylesbury,
Dublin 24.
Tel: 01-4514637
Humanistic & integrative; Gestalt, working with individuals, groups, supervision & trainer.
IAHIP

SKAR, Patricia
12 Brook Court,
Monkstown,
Co. Dublin.
Tel: 01-2300577
Jungian Analyst
IFPP

SKELTON, Ross
14 Gledswood Avenue,
Clonskeagh, Dublin 14.
Tel: 01-2697682
Psychoanalytic psychotherapy.
IFPP

SMITH, Ray
Group Analytic Practice,
Global House,
29 Lower Abbey Street, Dublin 1.
Tel: 01-8786486
Group analyst.
IGAS

SMITH, Susan
25 Glasnevin Hill,
Glasnevin, Dublin 9.
Tel: 01-8368966
Individuals, couples & family therapy.
FTAI

SMYTH, Geraldine
Eckhart House,
19 Clyde Road, Dublin 4.
Tel: 01-6606611 (H) / 6684687 (W)
Psychosynthesis/transpersonal.
IAHIP

SOMERS, Olive
Group Analytic Practice,
29 Lower Abbey Street, Dublin 1.
Tel: 01-8786486
Group analysis.
IGAS

SPARROW, Bobbie
Connect Assocs.,
Lonsdale House,
Avoca Avenue,
Blackrock, Co Dublin.
Tel: 01-4963784
Humanistic & integrative - individuals.
IAHIP

STEFANAZZI, Mary
Tel: 01-8686205
Humanistic from holistic & systemic perspective.
IAHIP

STEIN, Bernard N.
12 Ravens Way,
Prestwich,
Manchester M25 OEU, England.
Tel: 0161-7952898
Systemic, constructivist & humanistic & integrative. General adult & relationship & teenage problems.
IAHIP & FTAI

STONE, William
Stradbally,
Castleconnell, Co Limerick.
Tel: 061-315478
Humanistic & integrative psychotherapy.
IAHIP

SWEENEY, Brion
15 City Gate,
St Augustine Street, Dublin 8.
Tel: 01- 6707992/987
Constructivist/Humanistic integrative
IAHIP & ICPA

SWEENEY, Delma
1 Olney Mews,
Rathgar Avenue, Dublin 6.
Tel: 01-4966657
Humanistic integrative
IAHIP

SWEENEY, Patrick
Presbytery 2,
Dunmanus Road,
Cabra West,
Dublin 7.
Tel: 01-8389525
Systemic therapy
FTAI

TIERNEY, Aileen
Clanwilliam Institute,
18 Clanwilliam Terrace,
Dublin 2.
Tel: 01-6761363
Family therapy
FTAI

TIERNEY, Maggie
'Kilmoremoy'
Friarstown,
Ballyclough,
Co Limerick.
Tel: 061-229143
Humanistic & integrative
IAHIP

TONE, Yvonne
St Patrick's Hospital,
James' Street,
Dublin 8.
Tel: 01-6775423
Behavioural psychotherapy
CBT

TROOP, Deborah
31 Castle Park,
Monkstown,
Co Dublin.
Tel: 01-2806321
Humanistic relationship, dreams with Jungian perspective, small bodywork.
IAHIP & FTAI

TYRRELL, Patricia M.
Psychological Service, Dept. of Education,
Anne Street,
Wexford.
Tel: 053-24812
Systemic work in schools.
FTAI

UNDERWOOD-QUINN, Nicola

19 Sandymount Road,
Dublin 4.
Tel: 01-6684611
Individual, group, couple.
FTAI

VAN DOORSLAER, Mia

Vico Consultation Centre,
2 Dungar Terrace,
Off Northumberland Avenue,
Dun Laoghaire,
Co Dublin.
Tel: 01-2843336
The construction of 'problems' through language.
FTAI & ICPA

VAN HOUT, Els

Mount Scribe,
Kinvara,
Co Galway.
Tel: 091-637366
Biodynamic & integrative psychotherapy, personal totempole process, imagery work.
IAHIP

WALL MURPHY, Maura

2 Shanganagh Vale,
Loughlinstown, Co Dublin.
Tel: 01-2824024
Family therapy consultant mediator, mediation training.
FTAI

WALLACE, George

5 Castle Close,
Mahon,
Cork.
Tel: 021-358206
Gestalt therapy.
IAHIP

WALSH, Angela

324 Richmond Court,
Richmond Avenue South,
Dartry,
Dublin 6.
Tel: 01-4961039
Family therapy, couples & individual therapy.
FTAI

WALSH, Mary-Paula

Turning Point,
23 Crofton Road,
Dun Laoghaire,
Co Dublin.
Tel: 01-2800626 / 2807888
Individuals & families, consultancy training & supervision, life crises, bereavement & losses, life-threatening illnesses.
IAHIP & ICPA

WARD, Mary B.

Woodquay,
Galway.
Tel: 091-844148 /844209
Biodynamic & integrative psychotherapy.
IAHIP

WARD, Shirley A.

'Amethyst',
28 Beech Court,
Killiney, Co Dublin.
Tel: 01- 2862428 / 2850976
Eclectic: humanistic & integrative: pre- and perinatal psychotherapy.
IAHIP

WARDEN, Norman

Cnocan An Bhodaigh,
Furbo, Co Galway.
Tel: 091-591443
Integrative psychotherapy, anxiety, depression, unresolved grief, relationships.
IAHIP

WATSON, Patricia
Walmer House,
Raheny,
Co Dublin.
Tel: 01-8322472
Humanistic & integrative, including be-
reavement & mid-life transition.
IAHIP

WHITE, Joan
Dublin.
Tel: 01-2844044
Individual & couple therapy.
FTAI

WIECZOVEK-DEERING,
    Dorit
School of Social Sciences, Dublin,
Institute of Technology,
Rathmines House,
Dublin 6.
Tel: 01-4023509
Child & adolescent psychoanalytic psy-
chotherapy
IFCAP

WOODS, Jean
Dundalk Counselling Centre,
'Oakdene', 3 Seatown Place,
Dundalk,
Co Louth.
Tel: 042-38333
Humanistic & integrative, with specific
interest in serious illness/loss/grief.
IAHIP

WRIXON GOGGIN, Pauline
Aherina,
Kilmore,
Co Clare.
Tel: 061-473269
Humanistic & integrative psychothera-
pist, working with individuals & groups.
IAHIP

WYLIE-WARREN, Frances
Splaideog Cheille,
Keelty,
Drumcliffe,
Co Sligo.
Tel: 071-63694
Jungian analyst
IFPP

YOUNG, Anne
27 Rostrevor Road,
Rathgar,
Dublin 6
Tel: 01-4970331
Individual psychotherapy - Jungian/ana-
lytical.
IFPP

YOUNG, Sheilagh M.
2 The Coppins,
Foxrock,
Dublin 18.
Tel: 01-2892287
Family therapist.
FTAI.

PART IV

A Directory by County
of Psychotherapists in Ireland

For addresses and telephone numbers, please refer to the Directory section

ANTRIM
BENSON, Jarlath F.
HORNER, Carol

CARLOW
FADDEN, Rosaleen
SHEILL, Mary

CLARE
COLLINS, Geraldine
WRIXON GOGGIN,
 Pauline

CORK
AYLWIN, Susan
BRENNAN, Mairtine
BRIGHT, Jill
CONNOLLY, Brendan M.
BROWNE, Larry
DEVLIN, Fiona
DOYLE, Mary
ELLIS, Mary
FINLAYSON, Douglas
FLYNN, Stephen
GROVER, Mary Mrs.
HAMIL, Carmel
HARRINGTON, Eileen
HEALY, Daniel Christopher

HEALY, Donal
HERLIHY, Marie
JONES, Coleen
KELLIHER, Anne
LINDEN, Mairead
MARTIN, Ray
MC CASHIN, Dolores
MC GRATH, Terri
MELVIN PERREM, Breda
MOHALLY, Derry
MURRAY, Claire
O'CONNOR, Colm J.
O'LEARY, Eleanor
O'NEILL, Nora
RUTH-MURRAY, Ann M.
WALLACE, George

DONEGAL
CLANCY, Mary
DEENY, Peggy
DEVLIN, Teresa
FINNEGAN, Leo J.
MAGENIS, Maire
MC CARTHY, Dan
MC FADDEN, Hugh
MC GLYNN, Jim
MC GLYNN, Peter

MC GROARY-MEEHAN, Maureen
MC HUGH, Charles
MC LOONE, Anne
NANNERY, Teresa
SHERIDAN, Anne

DUBLIN

ANDREWS, Paul
ARNOLD, Mavis
ARTHURS, Mary
BAIRD, Jane
BARRY, Myra
BAYLY, Kathrin
BELTON, Mary W.
BERMINGHAM, Paula
BOLAND, Emille
BONFIELD, Dymphna
BOYLE, Martin
BOYNE, Edward
BREEN, Noreen
BROPHY, John
BURSTALL, Taru
BUTCHER, Gerard
BUTLER, Goretti
BUTLER, Maggie
BYRNE, Carmel
BYRNE, Mary
CADWELL, Nuala
CALLANAN, Fiodhna
CALLANAN, William Fr.
CAMPBELL, Carmel
CANAVAN, Mary
CARBERRY, Brian
CARR, Alan
CARROLL, Patricia

CARTON, Simone
CASEY, Grainne
CASSERLY, Felicity
CHILDERS, Nessa
CHOISEUL, Ann M.
CLAFFEY, Elaine
CLARKE, Margaret
CLARKE, Michele
COGHLAN, Helena
COLGAN, Patrick J.
COLLEARY, Maura
COLLINS, Deirdre
COLLINS, Ines
COLLINS, Mary
CONAGHAN, Mary
CONNOLLY, Margaret
CONROY, Kay
COX, Ann
COX CAMERON, Olga
DALY, Martin
DALY, Martin J.
DAVEY, Damien
DE BURCA, Bairbre
DE JONGH, Corry
DE LACY, Mara
DELMONTE, Michael M.
DENNEHY, Noreen
DONOGHUE, Mary
DONOHUE, Eugene
DOWD, Teresa
DOYLE, Rosaleen Mrs.
DOYLE, Sherry
DRISCOLL, Angela
DUFFY, Mary
DUGGAN, Colman
DWYER, Frankie-Ann

FAY, Joe
FERRITER, Kay
FINN, Monica
FITZGERALD, Barbara Mrs.
FLEMING, Pearl
FLEMING HOGAN, Bernie
FORBES, Jean
FOX, Michael
FOY, Emma
FRENCH, Gerry
FULTON, Linda
GAFFNEY, Delia
GALLIGAN, Patricia
GARLAND, Clive
GILL, Anne
GILL, Margaret
GILLILAND, Kay P.
GILMARTIN, Helen
GLEESON, Betty
GORDON, Evelyn
GRIMLEY, Carmel
GRINDLEY, Geraldine M.
GROSSMAN FREYNE, Gail
GUNNE, Dorothy
HARGIN, Mary Rose
HAUGHTON, Helen
HAYES, Fran
HEGARTY, Donal
HEGARTY, Owen
HOLLAND, Mary
HONNAY, Emiel
HOULIHAN, Tom
HOWARD, Leslie
HOWLET, Brian
HUMPHREYS, Vincent
HUNTER, Alison I.

JACKSON, Caitriona
JEBB, Winston
JENNINGS, Norman Fr
JONES, Helen
JOYCE, Nora
JUDGE, Jimmy
JUTHAN, Kay Mrs.
KEANE, Verena
KEARNEY, Philip
KEARNEY, Ruth
KEENAN, Marie
KEHOE, Helen
KELLEHER, Kathleen
KENNEDY, Jo
KILGALLEN, Aideen
KILLORAN-GANNON,
   Sheila
KOHNSTAMM, Barbara
KRZECZUNOWICZ,
   Sarah E. (Kay)
LESLIE, Frank
LEWIS, Maeve
LIDDY, Rosemary
LINDSAY, John
LINDSAY, Susan
LINNANE, Paul
LOGAN, Paddy
LOUGHLIN, Paula
LUCEY, Joe
LYNCH, Catherine
MACNAMARA, Vincent
MAGEE, David Louis
MAGUIRE, Una
MAHER, Bonnie
MAHER, Pascal
MANDOS, Koos

MANNION WALSHE,
  Deirdre
MASTERSON, Ingrid
MC CARTHY, Imelda
MC COURT, Ann
MC COURT, Marie
MC CULLY, Maria
MC GEE, Breda
MC GOLDRICK, Mary
MC HALE, Edmund
MC KEE, Maud
MC LEAVEY, Bernadette
MC LOUGHLIN, Sarah
MEAGHER, Kathleen A.
MEEK, Pauline
MOONEY, Alan A.
MOORE, Lucy M.
MULHERE, Jacinta
MULHOLLAND,
  Marie Therese
MULLER, Elizabeth
MURNANE, Eilis
MURPHY, Ann C.
MURPHY, Brendan
MURPHY, David
MURPHY, Ger
MURPHY, Mary
MURPHY ROCHE, Freda
MURRAY, Denis
MURRAY, Janet
MURRAY, Marie
NEARY, Nora
NÍ GHALLCHOBHAIR,
  Maighread
NÍ UALLACHÁIN, Meabh
NOLAN, Declan

NOLAN, Inger
NOLAN, Maeve
NOLAN, Patrick
O'BRIEN, David
O'BRIEN, Gay
O'BRIEN, Tom
O'BRIEN, Valerie
O'CONNOR, Elizabeth
O'CONNOR, Karen E.
O'CONNOR, Marika
O'DALAIGH, Liam
O'DEA, Catherine
O'DOHERTY, Colm
O'DONNELL, Godfrey
O'DONNELL, Ruth
O'DONOGHUE, Eilis
O'DONOGHUE, Jim
O'DONOGHUE, Paul
O'DONOVAN, Joan
O'DONOVAN, Margot
O'DUFFY, Ann
O'FLAHERTY, Anne
O'HALLORAN, Mary
O'HALLORAN, Mike
O'HANLON, Judy
O'HARA, Carmel
O'MAHONY, Eileen
O'MAHONY, Judy
O'MALLEY-DUNLOP, Ellen
O'NEILL, Mary
O'REILLY, Anne
O'REILLY, Maureen
O'ROURKE, Darina
O'SCOLLAIN, Eibhlin
O'SHAUGHNESSY, Marie
O'SULLIVAN, Marych

COUNTY DI

OWENS, Conor
PEAKIN, Anne
PHALAN, Sally
PORTER, Sheila
PRENDERVILLE, Mary
PRYLE, Fiona M.
PYLE, Mary
REYNOLDS, Mary
RICHARDSON, Anne
RIORDAN, Gillian Mrs
ROCHE, Declan
ROCHE, Sile
ROE, Liam
ROTHERY, Nuala
RUSSELL, Maura
RYAN, Anne
RYAN, Catherine
RYAN, David
RYAN, Derval
RYAN, Mairead
RYAN, Teresa
RYAN, Toni
SCULLY, Patricia
SHEEHAN, Bartley
SHEEHAN, Jim
SHIELDS, Vivienne
SHORTEN, Karen Ilean
SKAR, Patricia
SKELTON, Ross
SMITH, Ray
SMITH, Susan
SMYTH, Geraldine
SOMMERS, Olive
SPARROW, Bobbie
STEFANAZZI, Mary
SWEENEY, Brion
SWEENEY, Delma

SWEENEY, Patrick Fr.
TIERNEY, Aileen
TONE, Yvonne
TROOP, Deborah
UNDERWOOD-QUINN,
    Nicola
VAN DOORSLAER, Mia
WALL MURPHY, Maura
WALSH, Angela
WALSH, Mary-Paula
WARD, Shirley A.
WATSON, Patricia
WHITE, Joan
WIECZOVEK-DEERING,
    Dorit
YOUNG, Anne Mrs.
YOUNG, Sheilagh M.

FERMANAGH
MONAGHAN, Theresa

GALWAY
BREHONY, Rita
BUCKLEY, Marguerite
CONNEELY, Caitlin
CUNNINGHAM, Kathy
DENENY, Mary
DRISCOLL, Zelie
DUGGAN, Noel
FAHY, Michael
FRAWLEY, Angela
FRAWLEY, Michael
GRIEVE, Karin
HESKIN, Christina
KING, Margaret
MAHER, Ann
NÍ CHONAOLA, Mairead

NÍ NUALLÁIN, Mairin
O'MAHONY, Hank
O'NEILL, Breege
O'NEILL, Deborah
O'NEILL, Julia
SELL, Patrick
VAN HOUT, Els
WARD, Mary B.
WARDEN, Norman

KERRY
BYRNE, Patrick
KELLIHER, Anne
O'DOWD, Maura

KILDARE
CONNOLLY, Brendan
HARGIN, Mary Rose
HOWARD, Leslie
LALOR, Mary
MAC GUINNESS, Irene
MC CARTHY, Ros
SAHAFI, Janet E.

KILKENNY
MC GRATH, Terri
MOUNTAIN, Jane

LAOIS
BANNON, John
BERGIN, Alexander
FINGLETON, May
O'TOOLE, Muriel

LIMERICK
COLLINS-SMYTH,
  Margaret

CUNNINGHAM, Nora
MC ALEER, Jennifer
MC CARTHY, Anne
MYERS, Gerry
O'NEILL, Ann
STONE, William
TIERNEY, Maggie

LOUTH
BYRNE, Kathleen
BYRNE, Padraic
COSTELLO, Margaret
DEERY, Pat
DULLAGHAN, Elizabeth
  (Lillie)
DUNNE, Patricia
HAGAN, Patricia
HOWARD, Leslie
MOLEY, Patrick
O'BRIEN, Jim
PARKS, Ann
WOODS, Jean B.

MAYO
DUFFY, Kathleen
FORDE, Angela
O'DEA, Eileen

MEATH
DUFFY, Martin
KIRK, Geraldine
MC QUAID, Margaret

MONAGHAN
HUGHES, Maria

MATTHEWS, Peter
MC ADAM, Frank
REIDY, Margaret

OFFALY
O'DONOGHUE, Jim

ROSCOMMON
KEIGHER, Marian
KILCOYNE, Phyllis
LEE, Mary
MOYLAN, Bernadette
O'GRADY, Ethna
SHEEHAN, Thomas

SLIGO
BARRY, Kathleen
CURTIN, Geraldine
DOHERTY, Myra
HIRST, Iain
MC CARRICK, Tom
MC MORROW, Mary Mrs.
MONAGHAN, Ann Mrs.
MOONEY MC GLOIN,
   Catherine
MORRISON, Anne
NANNERY, Teresa
WYLIE-WARREN, Frances

TIPPERARY
BOURKE, Carmel
MADDEN, Joan
MARTIN, Maeve
MC MANUS, Libby
MURPHY, John P.
MYERS, Gerry

O'NEILL, Elizabeth
O'REILLY, Joseph

TYRONE
DEENY, Peggy

WATERFORD
BYRNE, Ruth
FRASER, Teresa
O'DONOVAN, Mairin
O'SULLIVAN, Creina

WESTMEATH
O'MAHONY, Catherine

WEXFORD
HILL, Rosemary
O'DWYER, Mary
TYRRELL, Patricia M.

WICKLOW
CARROLL, Patricia
DONNELLY, Pat
DUNNE, Ann Maria
KIERNAN, Donal
MAC NEILL, Sile

ENGLAND
FRENCH, Gerry
LONERGAN, Mary-Anna
RICHARDSON, Colette
STEIN, Bernard N.

CANADA
FOGARTY, Geraldine